Nikolai Sergeev

Half Ellipses

Nikolai Sergeev

Half Ellipses

A New Approach to Object Recognition

Südwestdeutscher Verlag für Hochschulschriften

Impressum / Imprint
Bibliografische Information der Deutschen Nationalbibliothek: Die Deutsche Nationalbibliothek verzeichnet diese Publikation in der Deutschen Nationalbibliografie; detaillierte bibliografische Daten sind im Internet über http://dnb.d-nb.de abrufbar.
Alle in diesem Buch genannten Marken und Produktnamen unterliegen warenzeichen-, marken- oder patentrechtlichem Schutz bzw. sind Warenzeichen oder eingetragene Warenzeichen der jeweiligen Inhaber. Die Wiedergabe von Marken, Produktnamen, Gebrauchsnamen, Handelsnamen, Warenbezeichnungen u.s.w. in diesem Werk berechtigt auch ohne besondere Kennzeichnung nicht zu der Annahme, dass solche Namen im Sinne der Warenzeichen- und Markenschutzgesetzgebung als frei zu betrachten wären und daher von jedermann benutzt werden dürften.

Bibliographic information published by the Deutsche Nationalbibliothek: The Deutsche Nationalbibliothek lists this publication in the Deutsche Nationalbibliografie; detailed bibliographic data are available in the Internet at http://dnb.d-nb.de.
Any brand names and product names mentioned in this book are subject to trademark, brand or patent protection and are trademarks or registered trademarks of their respective holders. The use of brand names, product names, common names, trade names, product descriptions etc. even without a particular marking in this works is in no way to be construed to mean that such names may be regarded as unrestricted in respect of trademark and brand protection legislation and could thus be used by anyone.

Coverbild / Cover image: www.ingimage.com

Verlag / Publisher:
Südwestdeutscher Verlag für Hochschulschriften
ist ein Imprint der / is a trademark of
AV Akademikerverlag GmbH & Co. KG
Heinrich-Böcking-Str. 6-8, 66121 Saarbrücken, Deutschland / Germany
Email: info@svh-verlag.de

Herstellung: siehe letzte Seite /
Printed at: see last page
ISBN: 978-3-8381-3140-5

Zugl. / Approved by: Uni Ulm, 2012

Copyright © 2012 AV Akademikerverlag GmbH & Co. KG
Alle Rechte vorbehalten. / All rights reserved. Saarbrücken 2012

Contents

1	**Introduction**	**3**
	1.1 Motivation	3
	1.2 Digital Image Preprocessing	4
	1.3 Architecture of an Object Recognition System	5
	1.3.1 Machine Learning Algorithms	5
	1.3.2 Representation	6
	1.4 Optical Flow Estimation	8
	1.5 Outline of Implementation	9
	1.5.1 Basic Idea	9
	1.5.2 Sketch of the Object Recognition System	10
	1.5.3 Sketch of the Flow Estimator	12
	1.6 Structure of the Thesis	14
2	**Machine Learning Algorithm**	**15**
	2.1 Introduction	15
	2.2 Core Algorithm	16
	2.3 Near Neighbor Search	21
	2.4 Properties of the Search Algorithm	23
3	**Form Description**	**25**
	3.1 Introduction	25
	3.2 Camera Model	29
	3.3 Combinations of Edges	35
	3.3.1 Rotation, Scaling, Translation Invariant Representation	35
	3.3.2 Reflection Invariance	39
	3.3.3 Projection Robustness	42
	3.4 Combinations of Half Ellipses	50
	3.4.1 Definition and Parametrization of a Half Ellipse	50
	3.4.2 Invariance	61
	3.4.3 Code Point Determination	62
	3.4.4 Code Point Velocity	67

		3.4.5	Code Point Net	70

4 Extraction of Half Ellipses   **71**
- 4.1 Basic Idea 71
- 4.2 Edge Detection 72
- 4.3 Line Detection 74
- 4.4 Making Line Chains 75
- 4.5 Detection of a Half Ellipse with Color 76

5 Flow Estimation   **79**

6 Experimental Results   **83**
- 6.1 Color Information 83
- 6.2 Object Recognition 83
  - 6.2.1 COIL-100 83
  - 6.2.2 Experiment Settings and Results 84
  - 6.2.3 Learning and Recognition Scheme Used for COIL-100 . 84
  - 6.2.4 Comparison to Alternative Approaches 85
- 6.3 Flow Estimation 86

7 Summary   **87**
- 7.1 Comparison to Other Methods 87
- 7.2 Conclusion 89

Glossary   **97**

Chapter 1

Introduction

1.1 Motivation

To build a visual perception system equivalent to the human one can be considered as the primary goal of computer vision. It is assumed there are two pathways of visual information processing in human cortex: the dorsal stream responsible for flow estimation and the ventral stream responsible for object recognition. If so, cortex solves every vision task through combination of object recognition and flow estimation. The approach to be introduced in this thesis also allows to build an object recognition system capable of flow estimation.

Here are some significant properties of the human visual perception system:

- robustness to affine transformations, partial occlusion and deformation
- capability to stable separation of a single object from its background or of several objects partially occluding each other
- capability to learn a new object in a time apparently independent of the number of objects already learned
- color information can be ignored or combined with form representation

The new method also has this characteristics. Nevertheless it still does not have some properties the cortex obviously has e.g. usage of texture for object recognition.

1.2 Digital Image Preprocessing

The very first step in image processing is normally noise reduction with some kind of filter described in [Jae05], [Dav05]. Practice shows that edge detection is far more stable afterwards. The most widespread edge detection algorithm for grayscale images was introduced by Canny [Can86] whose research was at least partially inspired by [Mar76], [MH80], [WG77]. After application of differential operator [Har80], [Pre70]the Canny algorithm thins out the resulting edge hills by using hysteresis thresholding. The Canny algorithm is a very powerful tool but the research on this area is still ongoing [SHS03] .

The system to be introduced in the thesis needs color on both sides of an edge to be extracted. Since Canny works with grayscale images some new technique of edge detection was necessary. The second reason to develop a new edge detector is general disability of differential operators to handle line lying near each other or sharp angles.

Usage of Hough transformation [Hou62], [Ros69], [DH72], [OC06] is a normal way of ellipse detection. However, as a global algorithm, the Hough transformation shares the issues of its class, namely detection of ellipses not visible for a human eye and therefore irrelevant for image understanding and poor detection of endpoints. These disadvantages inspired a new local half ellipse detection algorithm.

1.3 Architecture of an Object Recognition System

1.3.1 Machine Learning Algorithms

There are typically two kinds of object recognition systems: with or without a machine learning algorithm. A matching system e.g. SIFT [Low04], SURF [BETG08], general Hough transform [Bal81] uses no machine learning algorithm. Instead for example RANSAC [FB81] is used to find out the affine transformation. A matching algorithm compares an image to analyze with a single object at a time. For that reason it is not suitable for autonomic robotics.

Far more object recognition systems use some kind of machine learning algorithm. Such systems need feature vectors to represent an object. Boosting [FS97] is a simple and broadly used representative of machine learning algorithms. It is a binary classifier consisting of several "bad" binary classifiers. Nevertheless after being combined in a proper way these classifiers constitute a reliable and fast algorithm.

A support vector machine or SVM described in [Vap98], [CJT00], [SA02] is a widely used type of a machine learning algorithm. A single SVM is a binary classifier. Nevertheless several SVM's can be combined to build a classifier for more than just one class. The problem is that time demand to learn a new object depends e.g. linearly on the number of objects already learned. This makes the concept unsuitable for autonomic robotics.

A regression estimator [GKKW02] is a generalization of an SVM. A single regression estimator can be used to learn more than one class. The disadvantage of a regression estimator making it unsuitable for robotics is time demand to learn a new object. An estimator must be completely reconstructed with each new object to be learned.

The machine learning algorithm to be introduced in this thesis is an r-near neighbor search. An r-near neighbor algorithm looks for all feature vectors in storage similar enough to the query vector. The greatest advantage of such algorithms is its deterministic precision.

1.3.2 Representation

As the system to be introduced in this thesis interprets a 3D object as a set of 2D images, this section offers a short overview on the representation tactics of planar objects.

Fourier descriptors were initially described in [Rut70], [BP71]. The aim was to find rotation, translation, scaling invariant representation of a path-connected object. Affine invariant Fourier descriptors were described in [Arb90], [ASBH90]. Wavelets [TB97] are another way to represent a path-connected boundary of an object. General problem of the both methods is obviously the requirement of the path-connectedness of the boundary. There are plenty real world objects which do not satisfy this condition. Any way, it is still a challenge to extract the closed boundary loop of an object from a photo [KAT88]. Additionally, the methods are not robust enough to partial occlusion. A further problem is combination of color information with form representation.

Moments are another widespread method to represent an object. This technique was initially described in [Hu62]. In [Rei93] an attempt was made to make the representation invariant to affine transformations. The general problem of the method is its dependency on the gray scale values of the pixels belonging to the object. On the one hand, it cannot separate the color from the form, on the other hand, it does not really considers the color but the gray scale values. The technique is also not stable enough in handling partial occlusion.

Orientation histograms [DT05] are normally used to detect objects of one single class.

Reduction of an object to its skeleton [ACS81, PR67] helps to simplify it with its principal structure still being preserved.

Independent component analysis ICA [Com94],[HKO01] is used to normalize an object transformed through an affine mapping [SU11], [MA08]. ICA is tightly related with Principle Component Analysis PCA [Pea01], [Dun89], [FHT96] which is normally used to reduce the dimension of feature vectors. Usage of ICA requires segmentation of an object as a preprocessing step. Segmentation is a very complicated, ill-posed problem itself. The representation to be introduced in this thesis does not need object segmentation prior to its analysis.

Affine invariant point descriptors of planar objects [MZ92], [FMZ+91], [RZFM11], [SMP98] have one problem common to many feature based object descriptors: two objects having similar features do not have to appear similar for a human observer. Another problem is the absence of characteristic point e.g. in case of a circle. Nevertheless, the technique is still powerful enough

1.3. ARCHITECTURE OF AN OBJECT RECOGNITION SYSTEM

to be used for face recognition [KSHC94].

Representation of an object as a tree of characteristic points [Sam89a], [Sam89b] works stable enough if the 3D stance of an object and the distance to it are known. So it can be used only for industrial robotics.

1.4 Optical Flow Estimation

A typical flow estimator compares two frames and tries to allocate a translation vector to each pixel of the first frame showing its shift in the second frame. Ground truth fields of the Middlebury benchmark [BSL+07] are 2D arrays of the same size as the frames with 2D translation vectors as entries Figure 1.1. Such methods as Lucas-Kanade [LT81], [Luc84] or Horn-Schunck

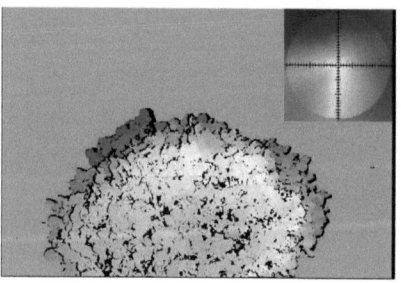

Figure 1.1: Ground truth of a flow estimation benchmark. The disk in the right upper corner explains the origin of the colors. It is based on HSV color space. Hue stands for the direction of the flow vector at a pixel. Saturation stands for the length of the flow vector at a pixel with white meaning vector length equal 0.

[HS81], [SRB10] work with gray scale images and and concentrate on the term

$$I_x(q)V_x + I_y(q)V_y + I_t(q) \tag{1.1}$$

with q pixel, $I_x(q), I_y(q), I_t(q)$ corresponding derivatives if the gray scale image I with respect to coordinates x, y and time t and flow vector V. V describes pixel translation and it has to be determined.

The new method looks not for corresponding points, at least not at the first step, but for corresponding half ellipses. The problem of flow propagation from half ellipses to the entire plane can be solved in an intuitive heuristic way. The method handles color images which is an advantage as from experience color is a powerful auxiliary tool. Further advantage of the new method is its capability to recognize rotation and scaling directly.

1.5 Outline of Implementation

1.5.1 Basic Idea

As the Figure 1.2 shows, the central idea of the system is to compare two combinations of half ellipses. It is to find out whether the combinations can be at least partially transformed into each other through an affine mapping. As the transformation can be partial, the system is robust to partial occlusion. The transformation does not have to be exact. If two combinations can be transformed into each other approximately with an error up to some ε-bound, they are regarded as similar by the system. The ε-error tolerance makes the system robust to deformation.

Figure 1.2: Two combinations, which can be exactly transformed into each other through reflection.

1.5.2 Sketch of the Object Recognition System

An object is represented as a set of half ellipse combinations A as shown in Figure 1.3. Combinations do not need to be of equal length.

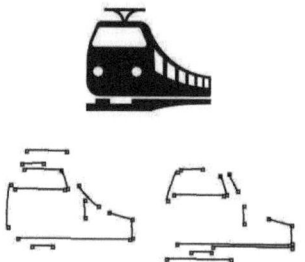

Figure 1.3: An object to learn and its representation.

For each $a \in A$ the system looks for a corresponding combination b in the image to analyze. b should be as long as possible.

Expressed more precisely: from the image to analyze the system extracts a set of half ellipses B as shown in Figure 1.4. For each combina-

Figure 1.4: An object to analyze with a set of extracted half ellipses.

tion $(a_i)_{i \in \{0,...,n\}} \in A$ a maximal $m \in \{1,...,n\}$ has to be determined for which a subsequence $\pi \in \{0,...,n\}^{\{0,...,m\}}$ with $\pi(0) = 0$ and $(b_i)_{i \in \{0,...,m\}} \in B^{\{0,...,m\}}$ exists so that $(a_{\pi(i)})_{i \in \{0,...,m\}}$ can be approximately transformed into $(b_i)_{i \in \{0,...,m\}}$ through translation, rotation, scaling, reflection and perspective change as shown in Figure 1.5. The overall number of combination pairs to

1.5. OUTLINE OF IMPLEMENTATION

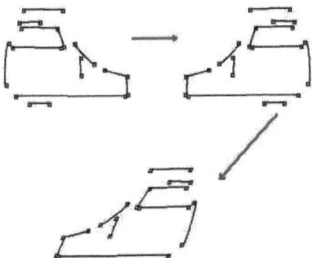

Figure 1.5: A way to transform one combination into anther.

be compared is
$$\sum_{(a_0,\ldots,a_n)\in A} \left(\sum_{m=1}^{n} \binom{n}{m} |B|^{m+1} \right). \tag{1.2}$$

With A containing only one combination of length $n = 10$ and B consisting of 50 half ellipses the number of pairs is at least 50^{10}.

As the system makes the check for each subsequence $(a_{\pi(i)})_{i\in\{0,\ldots,m\}}$ it is robust to partial occlusion.

Without any further extension this representation is color invariant.

1.5.3 Sketch of the Flow Estimator

The task of a dense flow estimator is to compare two frames and to allocate a translation vector to each pixel of the first one. The new method covers all edge points of the first frame with half ellipses Figures 1.6, 1.7. In the next step a set of combinations of half ellipses has to be constructed. For each combination the system looks for a corresponding combination in the second frame. In the last step the system propagates the flow from half ellipses to the entire plane.

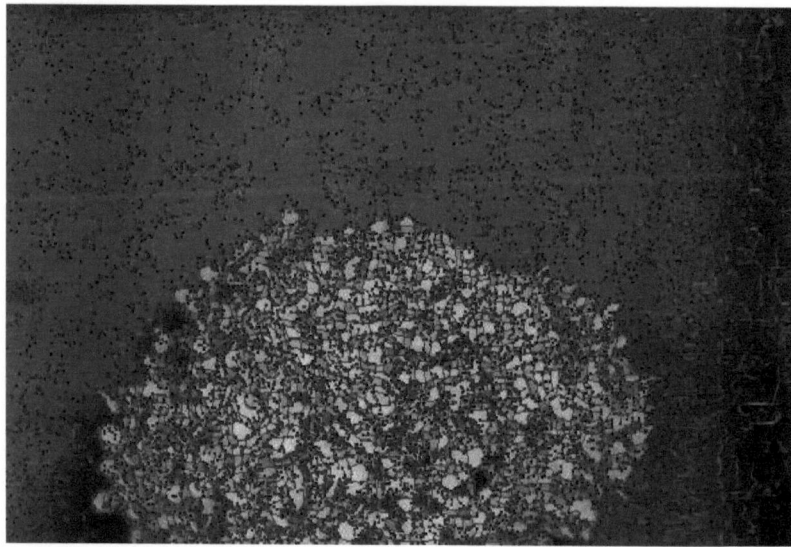

Figure 1.6: First frame and its detected half ellipses.

1.5. OUTLINE OF IMPLEMENTATION

Figure 1.7: Half ellipses of the first frame.

1.6 Structure of the Thesis

Chapter 2 describes the machine learning algorithm. The algorithm used for object recognition is built in two steps. In the first step a kernel algorithm is constructed. The final algorithm built in the second step is a trivial application case of the kernel algorithm. The task it solves is to find all stored vectors similar enough to the query vector with respect to maximum norm. As already mentioned it can be denoted as near neighbor search.

Chapter 3 introduces the object representation of the new approach. At first a representation of combinations of lines will be developed. It is rotation, translation, scaling and reflection invariant. It is also robust to partial occlusion and perspective change. Subsequently half ellipses and representation of half ellipse combinations will be described. The motivation to introduce the representation this way is to make it more comprehensible.

Chapters 3 and 2 are written in a more formal way as the other ones. On the one hand, this manner of description appears to be the most appropriate one for the issue of the chapter - on the other hand, the formal way of development of the new representation allowed to reduce the number of freely selectable system parameters.

Chapter 4 describes the way half ellipses can be extracted. It offers a new way of detection of edge points and lines. The new edge detection algorithm was designed to extract color on the both sides of a half ellipse. Striving to optimize the running time of line detection inspired the new line detection algorithm.

Chapter 5 contains a description of a rather trivial structure of the flow estimator built by means of the new approach. It describes the simplified representation of a combination of half ellipses and the trivial comparison algorithm related to the algorithm used for the object recognition.

Experimental results are shown in chapter 6. It consists of two parts dedicated to object recognition and flow estimation.

Chapter 7 basically discusses problems of the current implementation and suggests possible solution strategies.

Nontrivial mathematical statements made in this thesis have a formal proof. Trivial statements, which explicitly express an obvious mathematical idea and are needed for a proof or an implementation of an algorithm, may sometimes miss a formal justification. In general, absence of a proof of a lemma or a theorem in this thesis does not mean, a proof was not found yet - on the contrary, the corresponding proof is considered to be obvious.

Chapter 2

Machine Learning Algorithm

2.1 Introduction

The object representation to be introduced produces feature vectors which consist of similar permutable components. So it requires a machine learning algorithm invariant to possible permutations of components in a request feature vector. Unfortunately the standard machine learning algorithm as artificial neural networks [Ros62, Bis07], support vector machines [Vap98], regression estimators [GKKW02] or nearest neighborhood search algorithms [FH51] do not offer this property. Additionally, a machine learning algorithm feasible for robotics should be able to learn a new object in time as less dependent on the number of objects as possible. These two properties were the main motivation to develop the algorithm to be described in this chapter.

The new algorithm is a r-near neighbor search. For a given query it looks for all stored vectors lying in a r-ball around the query. The metrics used in this case is derived from supremum norm. A typical near neighbor search is either based on space partition [BKKS00] using e.g. Voronoi diagram or data partitioning [Gut00, CPZ97] using e.g. R-trees or M-trees. The core algorithm of the new search is based on space partitioning. The vector representation of the core algorithm is a spacial case of vector quantization [Pra01]. Classic vector quantization algorithms map a vector to a single subset of $\mathbb{R}^d$, whereas the new one maps a single vector to a set of subsets. Usually, a search space is partitioned in a finite number of subsets. The new representation uses an infinite partitioning, which results in a better performance and higher flexibility.

The description consists mainly of two parts. Part one introduces the core algorithm f. Part two shows the implementation of the actual machine learning algorithm F used for the object recognition.

In this thesis it will be assumed that time complexity of saving and accessing of an element of hash map is independent of the number of elements already saved. It simplifies running time calculation omitting unnecessary details.

2.2 Core Algorithm

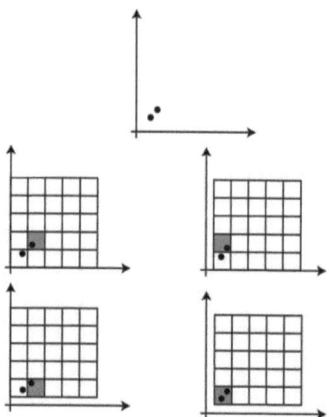

Figure 2.1: Point encoding in $\mathbb{R}^2$.

The basic idea is to represent a point in $\mathbb{R}^d$ as a set of cuboids. Figure 2.1 shows how two points get encoded in $\mathbb{R}^2$. Each of them is represented by four cuboids. As they are similar enough to each other with respect to supremum norm they share at least one cuboid.

For $d, K \in \mathbb{N}, \varepsilon > 0$ and a sequence of vectors $v \in \prod_{k \in \{1,...,K\}} \mathbb{R}^d$ the function $f : \mathbb{R}^d \to P(\{1, ..., K\})$ with

$$f(x) = \{k \leq K \mid \|x - v_k\|_{\max} \leq \varepsilon\} \tag{2.1}$$

has to be implemented. The following interpretation of v makes the definition of f comprehensible: $v_k \in \mathbb{R}^d$ is an encoded description vector of the label $k \in \{1, ..., K\}$. $f(x)$ returns all labels whose code is similar to x. In this section a fast implementation of f will be described.

At first several encoding functions E^i with $i \in \{1, ..., 6\}$ are to be introduced. The $E^1, ..., E^5$ are auxiliary functions used to define E^6.

2.2. CORE ALGORITHM

Definition 2.1 *For $\delta > 0$ the encoder $E_\delta^1 : \mathbb{R} \to \mathbb{Z}$ is defined as*

$$E_\delta^1(x) = \left\lceil \frac{x}{\delta} \right\rceil. \tag{2.2}$$

with $\lceil \cdot \rceil$ standing for ceiling function.

For example $E_\delta^1(0) = 0$ for all $\delta > 0$.

Definition 2.2 *The encoder $E_\delta^2 : \mathbb{R} \to \mathbb{Z}$ is defined as*

$$E_\delta^2(x) = E_\delta^1\left(x + \frac{\delta}{2}\right). \tag{2.3}$$

For example $E_\delta^2(0) = 1$ with $\delta > 0$.

Definition 2.3 *The encoder $E_\delta^3 : \mathbb{R} \to \mathbb{Z}^2$ is defined as*

$$E_\delta^3(x) = \left(2E_\delta^1(x), 2E_\delta^2(x) + 1\right)^T. \tag{2.4}$$

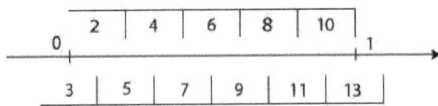

Figure 2.2: Mapping behavior of $2E_{1/5}^1(\cdot)$ (above the axis) and $2E_{1/5}^2(\cdot) + 1$ (under the axis)

Obviously $E_\delta^3(0) = (0, 3)^T$.

Definition 2.4 *The encoder $E_{d,\delta}^4 : \mathbb{R}^d \to \mathbb{Z}^{2 \times d}$ is defined as*

$$E_{d,\delta}^4(x) = \left(\left(E_\delta^3(x_j)\right)_i\right)_{(i,j) \in \{1,2\} \times \{1,\ldots,d\}}. \tag{2.5}$$

For $d = 3$ and $x = (0, 0, 0)^T$ $E_{d,\delta}^4(x) = \begin{pmatrix} 0 & 0 & 0 \\ 3 & 3 & 3 \end{pmatrix}$.

Definition 2.5 *The encoder $E_{d,\delta}^5 : \mathbb{R}^d \times \{1, 2\}^d \to \mathbb{Z}^d$ is defined as*

$$E_{d,\delta}^5(x, y) = \left(\left(E_{d,\delta}^4(x)\right)_{y(i),i}\right)_{i \in \{1,\ldots,d\}}. \tag{2.6}$$

For example $E_{d,\delta}^5(x, y) = (0, 3, 0)^T$ with $d = 3, x = (0, 0, 0)^T$ and $y = (1, 2, 1)^T$. An outcome of $E_{d,\delta}^5(x, y)$ will be typically referred as sample.

Definition 2.6 *The encoder* $E_{d,\delta}^6 : \mathbb{R}^d \to P(\mathbb{Z}^d)$ *is defined as*

$$E_{d,\delta}^6(x) = \left\{ E_{d,\delta}^5(x,y) \middle| y \in \{1,2\}^d \right\}. \tag{2.7}$$

To implement $f(x) = \{k \leq K | \ \|x - v_k\|_{\max} \leq \varepsilon\}$ the following type of storage $s : \mathbb{Z}^d \to P(\{1,...,K\})$ has to be defined

$$s(x) = \left\{ k \in \{1,...,K\} \middle| x \in E_{d,\delta}^6(v_k) \right\} \tag{2.8}$$

with $\delta = 2\varepsilon$. In Java notation the storage can be implemented as follows:

```
Map<List<Integer>, Set<Integer>> s =
    new HashMap<List<Integer>, Set<Integer>>();
for (int k = 1; k <= K; k++)
    for (List<Integer> y : E^6_(d, delta)(x))
        if (s.containsKey(y))
            s.get(y).add(k);
        else {
            s.put(y, new HashSet<Integer>());
            s.get(y).add(k);
        }
```

Finally $f(x)$ can be implemented.

Task 2.1 *Implement* $f(x) = \{k \leq K | \ \|x - v_k\|_{\max} \leq \varepsilon\}$. *The algorithm should be denoted as* $A_{\varepsilon,d}^1$.

Implementation: The algorithm can be realized as

$$A_{\varepsilon,d}^1(x) = \left\{ k \in \bigcup_{y \in E_{d,\delta}^6(x)} s(y) \ \middle| \ \|x - v_k\|_{\max} \leq \varepsilon \right\}. \tag{2.9}$$

This implementation can be encoded in the following way:

```
Set<Integer> f(x) = new HashSet<Integer>();
for (List<Integer> y : E^6_{d, delta}(x))
    for (Integer k : s.get(y))
        if (|| x - v_k ||_max <= epsilon)
            f(x).add(k);
```

$\square$

It remains to prove the ensuing theorem.

Theorem 2.1 *For* $x \in \mathbb{R}^d$ *we have*

$$f(x) = A_{\varepsilon,d}^1(x).$$

2.2. CORE ALGORITHM

The theorem can be formulated as the following statement:

$$\|x - v_k\|_{\max} \leq \varepsilon \Rightarrow k \in \bigcup_{y \in E^6_{d,\delta}(x)} s(y) \tag{2.10}$$

and

$$k \in \bigcup_{y \in E^6_{d,\delta}(x)} s(y) \Rightarrow \|x - v_k\|_{\max} \leq 2\varepsilon. \tag{2.11}$$

To prove the statement we need the following lemmas. Except for the first lemma they are of trivial nature and do not need an explicit proof.

Lemma 2.1 *For $\varepsilon > 0$ set $\delta = 2\varepsilon$. Then we have:*

$$\forall x, y \in \mathbb{R} : |x - y| \leq \varepsilon \Rightarrow E^1_\delta(x) = E^1_\delta(y) \vee E^2_\delta(x) = E^2_\delta(y)$$

Proof: It's enough to show that

$$E^1_\delta(x) \neq E^1_\delta(y) \wedge |x - y| \leq \varepsilon \Rightarrow E^1_\delta\left(x + \frac{\delta}{2}\right) = E^1_\delta\left(y + \frac{\delta}{2}\right).$$

For $n_x = E^1_\delta(x)$ and $n_y = E^1_\delta(y)$ we will see at first

$$|n_x - n_y| \leq 1.$$

Considering

$$n_x - 1 < \frac{x}{\delta} \leq n_x$$
$$\wedge$$
$$n_y - 1 < \frac{y}{\delta} \leq n_y \Leftrightarrow -n_y \leq -\frac{y}{\delta} < -n_y + 1$$

we get

$$n_x - n_y - 1 \leq \frac{x - y}{\delta} \leq n_x - n_y + 1$$

$$\Rightarrow -1\frac{1}{2} \leq -1 + \frac{x-y}{\delta} \leq n_x - n_y \leq \frac{x-y}{\delta} + 1 \leq 1\frac{1}{2}.$$

Now it will be shown

$$E^1_\delta\left(x + \frac{\delta}{2}\right) = E^1_\delta\left(y + \frac{\delta}{2}\right).$$

Without loss of generality assume $x < y$.

$$\frac{y}{\delta} - n_x \leq \frac{y}{\delta} - \frac{x}{\delta} \leq \frac{1}{2} \Rightarrow \frac{y}{\delta} + \frac{1}{2} \leq n_x + 1 = n_y$$

$$n_x - \frac{x}{\delta} < \frac{y}{\delta} - \frac{x}{\delta} \leq \frac{1}{2} \Rightarrow n_x < \frac{x}{\delta} + \frac{1}{2}$$

□

Lemma 2.2 *For $\delta > 0$ we get*

$$\forall x, y \in \mathbb{R} : E_\delta^1(x) = E_\delta^1(y) \vee E_\delta^2(x) = E_\delta^2(y) \Rightarrow |x - y| \leq \delta.$$

Lemma 2.3 *For $d \in \mathbb{N}, \varepsilon > 0$ set $\delta = 2\varepsilon$. Then we have*

$$\forall x, y \in \mathbb{R}^d : \|x - y\|_{\max} \leq \varepsilon \Rightarrow E_{d,\delta}^6(x) \cap E_{d,\delta}^6(y) \neq \emptyset.$$

Lemma 2.4 *For $d \in \mathbb{N}, \delta > 0$ we have*

$$\forall x, y \in \mathbb{R}^d : E_{d,\delta}^6(x) \cap E_{d,\delta}^6(y) \neq \emptyset \Rightarrow \|x - y\|_{\max} \leq \delta.$$

All $k \in \{1, ..., K\}$ with $\|x - v_k\|_{\max} \leq \varepsilon$ are definitely contained in the preliminary response $\bigcup_{y \in E_{d,\delta}^6(x)} s(y)$. But for some $k \in \bigcup_{y \in E_{d,\delta}^6(x)} s(y)$ one still has $\varepsilon < \|x - v_k\|_{\max} \leq 2\varepsilon$. Such $k \in \{1, ..., K\}$ have to be sifted out through explicit check $\|x - v_k\|_{\max} \leq \varepsilon$. Though not similar enough wrong v_k are still pretty similar to x. For that reason the number of false positives cannot be too large in an average case. It is important for the running time of the algorithm. The trivial implementation of $f : \mathbb{R}^d \to P(\{1, ..., K\})$ makes the explicit check $\|x - v_k\|_{\max} \leq \varepsilon$ for all $k \in \{1, ..., K\}$. The introduced algorithm makes the explicit comparison only for such v_k, which are pretty similar to x in sense of $\|x - v_k\|_{\max} \leq 2\varepsilon$. This aspect is responsible for the acceleration of $f(x)$ calculation.

The calculation of $f(x)$ consists of two parts. Part one determines the set of samples $E_{d,\delta}^6(x)$. Part two checks for all elements of $\{k \in s(y) | y \in E_{d,\delta}^6(x)\}$ if $\|x - v_k\|_{\max} \leq \varepsilon$ and adds k if necessary to $f(x)$. The time demand to calculate $E_{d,\delta}^6(x)$ is $O(2^d)$ and independent of K. The time demand of the second part is obviously $C|\{k \in s(y) | y \in E_{d,\delta}^6(x)\}|$. But all learned labels $\{1, ..., K\}$ are evenly distributed among millions of possible samples. For that reason $|s(y)|$ of a single sample $y \in E_{d,\delta}^6$ is small. Therefore $\{k \in s(y) | y \in E_{d,\delta}^6(x)\}$ is small. Time demand for a single check $\|x - v_k\|_{\max} \leq \varepsilon$ and addition to $f(x)$ is also small. All in all the implementation of $f(x)$ is fast.

Storage space demand estimation is trivial for this algorithm. In the worst case to save a new $v_k \in \mathbb{R}^d$ one needs 2^d sample vectors $y \in E_{d,\delta}^6(x) \subseteq \mathbb{Z}^d$ and 2^d copies of the label k, one for each sample. Space complexity is obviously linear to the number of saved vectors v_k. In big O notation it is $O((2^d d + 2^d)K) = O(2^d dK)$. The time demand to store an additional vector v_k is independent of the number of the vector already saved K. In other words it is $O(1)$.

Running time of $f(x)$-calculation depends on $\max_{x \in \mathbb{Z}^d} |s(x)|$. Assuming v_k evenly distributed over entire $\mathbb{R}^d$ we get a finite set of K labels distributed over infinitely many samples from $\mathbb{Z}^d$. In this purely theoretical situation the running time does not change with growing K in an probabilistically average case. Experiments show that for the new approach the running time depends linearly on the number of learned feature vectors.

2.3 Near Neighbor Search

Let $FS = \{X \in P(\mathbb{R}^d) | |X| < \infty\}$ denote the set of finite subsets of $\mathbb{R}^d$. The function
$$F : FS \to \mathbb{N} \times P(\mathbb{N}) \tag{2.12}$$
to be implemented in this section is closely related to the previous one. It analyzes not just a single vector but a set of vectors. To construct f a sequence of vectors $(v_k)_{k \in \{1,...,K\}} \subseteq \mathbb{R}^d$ is used - for F a sequence of combinations $(c_k)_{k \in \{1,...,K\}}$ of such vectors with
$$c_k \in \underbrace{\mathbb{R}^d \times ... \times \mathbb{R}^d}_{l_k} \tag{2.13}$$
and $l_k \in \mathbb{N}$ length of each combination. c_k don't have to be of equal length. Now $F(X)$ with $X \in FS$ will be defined in several steps. For each $k \in \{1,...,K\}$ let $m_k \in \mathbb{N}_0$ denote the maximal integer, for which a subsequence $\pi : \{1,...,m_k\} \to \{1,...,l_k\}$ and a combination $x \in X^{m_k}$ exist with
$$\max_{i \in \{1,...,m_k\}} \|c_{\pi(i)} - x_i\|_{\max} \le \varepsilon. \tag{2.14}$$
For $M = \max_{k \in \{1,...,K\}} m_k$ the function $F : FS \to \mathbb{N} \times P(\mathbb{N})$ is defined as
$$F(X) = (M, \{k \in \{1,...,K\} | m_k = M\}). \tag{2.15}$$
The storage s needed to implement F is built in the following way:

```
Map<List<Integer>, Map<Integer, Set<Integer>>> s =
    new HashMap<List<Integer>, Map<Integer, Set<Integer>>>();

for (int k = 1; k <= K; k++) \\ number of combination
    for (int i = 1; i <= l_k; i++)\\ number of component
        for (List<Integer> x : E^6_{d, delta}(c_k(i)))
            if (s.containsKey(x))
                if (s.get(x).containsKey(i))
                    s.get(x).get(i).add(k);
                else {
                    s.get(x).put(i, new HashSet<Integer>());
                    s.get(x).get(i).add(k);
```

```
        }
        else {
            s.put(x, new HashMap<Integer, Set<Integer>>());
            s.get(x).put(i, new HashSet<Integer>());
            s.get(x).get(i).add(k);
        }
```

Task 2.2 *Implement $F(X)$. The algorithm should be denoted as $A^2_{\varepsilon,c}$.*

Implementation: $F(X)$ can be implemented in the following way:

```
Map<Integer, Set<Integer>> sub = new HashMap<Integer, Set<Integer>>();
\\ recognized subcombinations
\\ Integer k in sub.get(k) stands for
\\ the number of recognized combination
\\ Integer i element of Set<Integer>
\\ sub.get(k) stands for the number of
\\ recognized component
for (List<Double> x : X)
    for (List<Integer> y : E^6_{d, delta}(x))
        if (s.containsKey(y))
            for (Integer i : s.get(x).keySet())
                for (Integer k : s.get(i))
                    if (||x - c_k(i)||_max <= epsilon)
                        if (sub.containsKey(k))
                            sub.get(k).add(i);
                        else {
                            sub.put(k, new HashSet<Integer>());
                            sub.get(k).all(i);
                        }
Map<Integer, Integer> m = new HashMap<Integer, Integer>();
for (Integer k : sub.keySet())
    m.put(k, sub.keySet.size());
```

After having gained m_k the remaining part of implementation is trivial.

$\square$

Replacing K through $N = \sum_{k=1}^{K} l_k$ in the estimation of space complexity of the first implementation one gains corresponding estimations for the second implementation: $O(2^d dN)$. Theoretical run time complexity is still $O(1)$, empirical - $O(N)$.

2.4 Properties of the Search Algorithm.

This chapter presented a new near neighbor search algorithm. There are some interesting properties of the algorithm resulting immediately from the definition, which are worth to be mentioned. Time demand to learn a new vector is independent of the number of vectors already learned. It makes the algorithm suitable for robotics. A query gets processed with 100% precision. High dimensional vectors consisting of similar components can be handled. Admittedly time complexity grows exponentially to the size of a single component but at the same time just linearly to the number of components in a single query vector. Another property of the algorithm is its robustness to the partial occlusion. Components can be cut out - the algorithm still recognizes the remaining part. Under artificial and purely theoretical conditions time demand to process a single query vector does not change with the number of stored vectors.

Chapter 3

Form Description

3.1 Introduction

The purpose of this chapter is to introduce a new half ellipse based form representation which is invariant to rotation, translation, scaling, reflection and robust to perspective change as well as partial occlusion. The new form representation will be introduced in two steps. In the first step - the representation of a combination of edges in Section 3.3. In the second step - the representation of a combination of half ellipses in Section 3.4. A line is a half ellipse. So a half ellipse combination is a generalization of a line combination. Its representation is enlarged with the bow of half ellipse. The introduction is structured that way just to make the architecture of the feature vectors more comprehensible.

As already mentioned, the representation should be rotation, translation, scaling (Subsection 3.3.1 and 3.4.1) and reflection (Subsection 3.3.2) invariant. Based on this representation there will be built a system robust to perspective change in Subsection 3.3.3 and 3.4.5. Figure 3.1 shows how endpoints of a half ellipses are encoded invariantly to rotation, translation and scaling. The representation code can directly read out from the right part of the image. Points (a, b, c, d, e, f) are represented by (a', b', c', d', e', f').

Reflection invariance means independence of the representation from the axis of mirroring. There are infinitely many axes. Figure 3.2 shows two of them: horizontal and vertical. The reflection invariant representation of a single combination consists of two feature vectors: the old one Figure 3.1 and the new one visualized in Figure 3.3. Both combinations from Figure 3.2 produce the same representation vector shown in Figure 3.3.

Figure 3.4 visualizes the formulation and implementation of the perspective robustness. The task is to recognize an object (red rectangular) if the

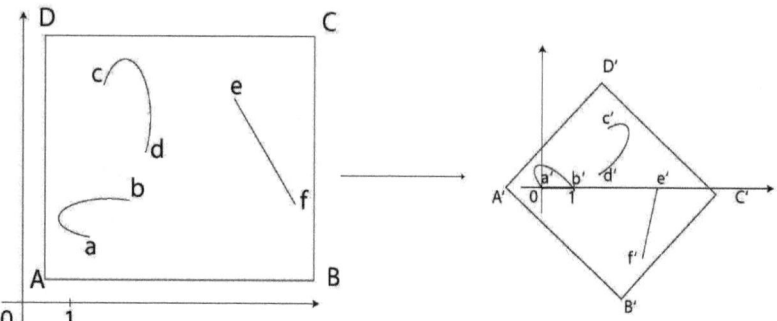

Figure 3.1: Representation of the endpoints of a combination.

camera is at some point above the black line with projection surface parallel to the tangential plane of the hemisphere at the point. The basic idea of the implementation is to find an in some sense minimal coverage of the area above the black line, to transform the original translation, reflection, scaling and reflection invariant representation for each quadrant and to learn it.

3.1. INTRODUCTION

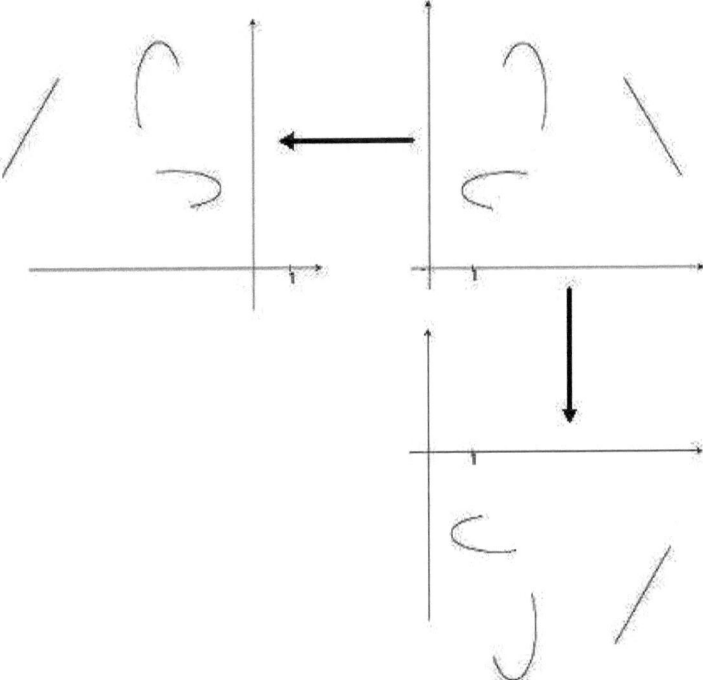

Figure 3.2: Two reflection axes. The original image is in the right upper corner; the image after the horizontal reflection - in the left upper corner; the image after vertical reflection - in the right lower corner.

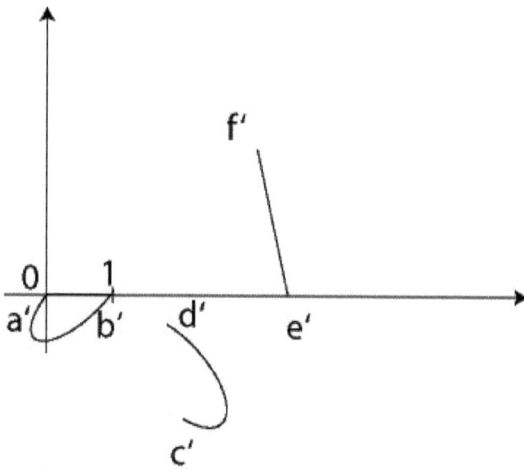

Figure 3.3: Visualization of the second reflection invariant representation vector. (a', b', c', d', e', f') represents endpoints of the both reflected combinations of the Figure 3.2.

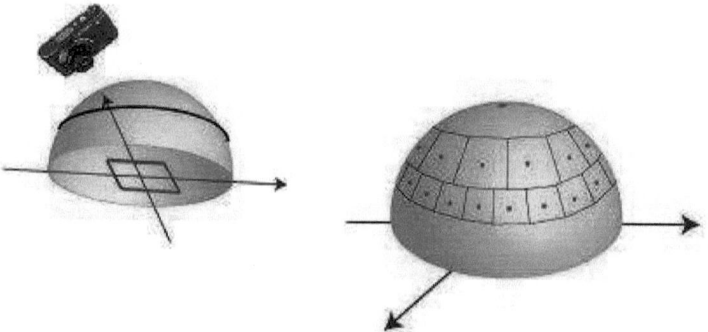

Figure 3.4: Formulation and implementation of the perspective robustness.

3.2 Camera Model

The system to be introduced should become robust to the perspective change of a camera. The camera model used in the system consists of two parts. Part one describes the transformation of a planar object in camera coordinates when camera changes its point of view. Part two describes the projection of a space point to the camera surface.

A new camera model was needed to handle positioning of the camera at the perspective hemisphere Figure 3.4 in a way which would allow to integrate it in further mathematical analysis. There are mainly two reasons why the new model appears to be appropriate. It is linear and it reduces the 3D process of camera positioning to a 2D mapping unlike e.g. pinhole projection.

The model to be introduced lives within camera coordinates. The purpose is to show that the linear mapping

$$\begin{pmatrix} \sin\alpha & 0 \\ 0 & 1 \end{pmatrix} \begin{pmatrix} \cos\beta & -\sin\beta \\ \sin\beta & \cos\beta \end{pmatrix} \qquad (3.1)$$

with $\alpha \in (0, \pi/2]$, $\beta \in \mathbb{R}$ is a proper tool to model the two transformations.

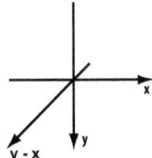

Figure 3.5: $(y - x)$-axis.

At first $(y - x)$-axis has to be introduced. As shown in Figure 3.5 $y - x$-axis lies in (x, y)-plane. It emerges through subtracting the y-axis from the x-axis.

Let the rectangle $ABCD$ denote the projection surface of the camera. The rectangle $EFGH$ denotes the object to be mapped on the projection surface of the camera. The Figure 3.6 shows the initial position of the camera and the object in space coordinates. Both planes are parallel to each other. The projection plane of the camera is at the summit of the perspective hemisphere.

To denote a point on a sphere the spherical coordinate system is used. A

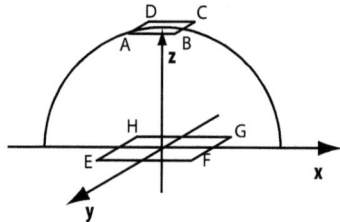

Figure 3.6: Initial position of the camera $ABCD$ and the object $EFGH$ in space coordinates.

point $(x, y, z)^T \in \mathbb{R}^3$ is described through $(\beta, \alpha, r)^T \in \mathbb{R}^3$ as

$$\begin{pmatrix} \beta \\ \alpha \\ r \end{pmatrix} \mapsto \begin{pmatrix} r \cos \alpha \cos \beta \\ r \cos \alpha \sin \beta \\ r \sin \alpha \end{pmatrix} = \begin{pmatrix} x \\ y \\ z \end{pmatrix} \qquad (3.2)$$

Figure 3.7 shows the position of a point on hemisphere with $\alpha, \beta = 45°$. Figure 3.8 shows the positioning process of the camera at the point $\alpha, \beta = 45°$ viewed from above. Figure 3.9 shows the last step of positioning of the camera at the point $\alpha, \beta = 45°$ viewed askance. Figure 3.10 shows an obvious alternative positioning of the camera at the point $\alpha, \beta = 45°$ viewed from above. Figure 3.11 shows the last step of the alternative positioning of the camera at the point $\alpha, \beta = 45°$ viewed askance. In the last step the alternative camera positioning will be described in camera coordinates. Figure 3.12 shows the initial camera\object position in camera coordinates.

Figures 3.13 and 3.14 show the positioning of the camera at the point $\alpha, \beta = 45°$ in 3D and viewed from above respectively.

The images show that the mapping 3.1 with $\alpha \in (0, \pi/2]$ and $\beta \in \mathbb{R}$ describes the transformation of x, y coordinates of an object point in camera coordinates when the camera changes its position at the hemisphere. The transformation of z coordinate is described with

$$z \mapsto z - \cos \alpha (\cos \beta x - \sin \beta y). \qquad (3.3)$$

The second part of the camera model describes the projection of a space point on the camera surface. Intuitively pin hole projection seems to be

3.2. CAMERA MODEL

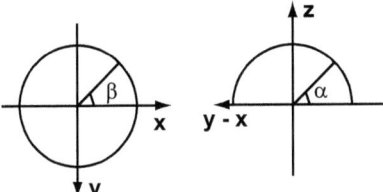

Figure 3.7: Illustration of the position of a point on hemisphere with $\alpha, \beta = 45°$.

a natural candidate to realize this part of the model. However pin hole transformation is not linear and subsequently quite difficult to handle mathematically. For that reason it is a common approach in affine invariant object recognition to approximate pin hole projection with parallel projection

$$\begin{pmatrix} x \\ y \\ z \end{pmatrix} \mapsto \begin{pmatrix} x \\ y \end{pmatrix} \qquad (3.4)$$

as the images are similar if the ratio of the distance of a camera to an object to the smallest radius of a ball enclosing the object is big.

As the z coordinate plays no role in modeling the perspective change of a camera it is possible to describe the 3D process of camera relocation through 2D mapping 3.1.

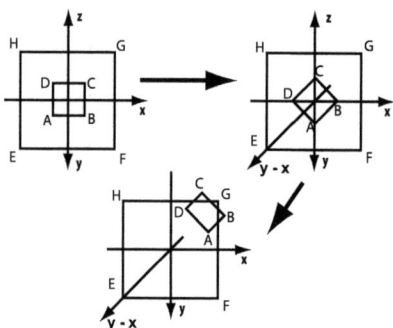

Figure 3.8: Positioning of the camera at the point $\alpha, \beta = 45°$ viewed from above.

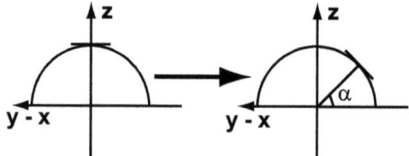

Figure 3.9: The last step of positioning of the camera at the point $\alpha, \beta = 45°$ viewed askance.

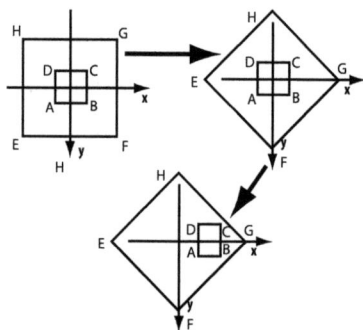

Figure 3.10: Alternative positioning of the camera at the point $\alpha, \beta = 45°$ viewed from above.

3.2. CAMERA MODEL

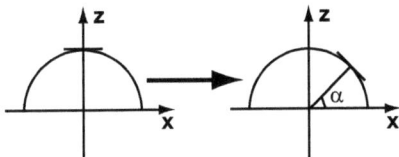

Figure 3.11: Last step of the alternative positioning of the camera at the point $\alpha, \beta = 45°$ viewed askance.

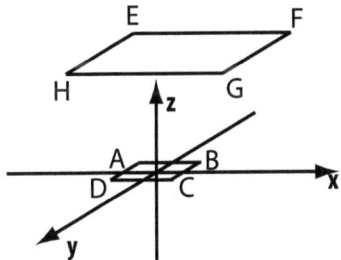

Figure 3.12: Initial camera\object position in camera coordinates.

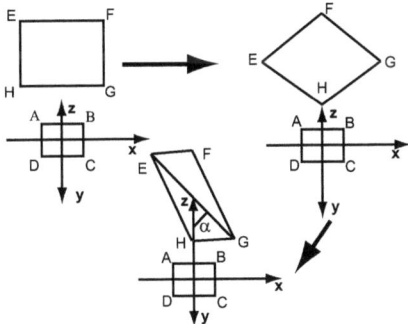

Figure 3.13: Positioning of the camera at the point $\alpha, \beta = 45°$ in camera coordinates.

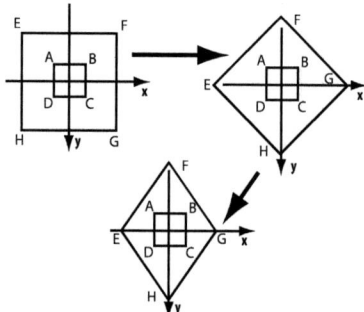

Figure 3.14: Positioning of the camera at the point $\alpha, \beta = 45°$ in camera coordinates viewed from above.

3.3. COMBINATIONS OF EDGES

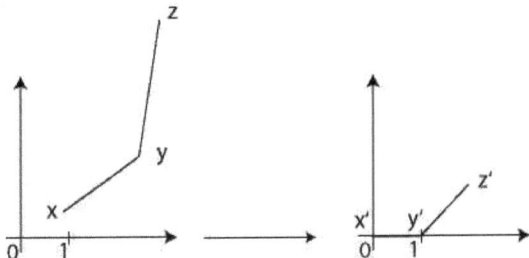

Figure 3.15: Visualization of $F^2_{x,y}(z)$.

3.3 Combinations of Edges

3.3.1 Rotation, Scaling, Translation Invariant Representation

This subsection describes a way to represent a combination of edges invariant to rotation, scaling and shifting. The entire combination gets encoded relatively to the first edge. The central tool of this representation is function F^1, which encodes one edge relatively to another one. The representation of a combination comes up through iterative application of the function on the first edge of the combination and other edges of the combination. At the end a simple object recognition system based on this representation will be build.

In this thesis the set $\mathbb{R}^2$ and the complex plane $\mathbb{C}$ are considered as identical.

Definition 3.1 *For $x \in \mathbb{R}^2 \backslash \{0\}$ the function F^1_x is defined as follows:*

$$F^1_x : \begin{cases} \mathbb{R}^2 \to \mathbb{R}^2 \\ y \mapsto F^1_x(y) = \frac{1}{x_1^2 + x_2^2} \begin{pmatrix} x_1 & x_2 \\ -x_2 & x_1 \end{pmatrix} \begin{pmatrix} y_1 \\ y_2 \end{pmatrix} \end{cases}$$

Figure 3.15 visualizes the mapping behavior of F^1.

Lemma 3.1 *For $(x, y) \in \mathbb{C} \backslash \{0\} \times \mathbb{C}$ we get*

$$F^1_x(y) = \frac{y}{x}.$$

Definition 3.2 For $x, y \in \mathbb{R}^2, x \neq y$ the function $F^2_{x,y}$ is defined as follows:

$$F^2_{x,y} : \begin{cases} \mathbb{R}^2 \to \mathbb{R}^2 \\ z \mapsto F^1_{y-x}(z - x) \end{cases}$$

Definition 3.3 For $a \in \mathbb{R}^2, \beta \in \mathbb{R}, \gamma \in (0, \infty)$ translation T_a, rotation R_β and scaling S_γ are defined as follows:

$$T_a : \begin{cases} \mathbb{R}^2 \to \mathbb{R}^2 \\ x \mapsto x + a \end{cases}$$

$$R_\beta : \begin{cases} \mathbb{R}^2 \to \mathbb{R}^2 \\ x \mapsto \begin{pmatrix} \cos\beta & -\sin\beta \\ \sin\beta & \cos\beta \end{pmatrix} \begin{pmatrix} x_1 \\ x_2 \end{pmatrix} \end{cases}$$

$$S_\gamma : \begin{cases} \mathbb{R}^2 \to \mathbb{R}^2 \\ x \mapsto \gamma x \end{cases}$$

Lemma 3.2 For $x, y \in \mathbb{C}$ with $x \neq y$ and $z \in \mathbb{C}$ we get

$$\forall a \in \mathbb{C} : F^2_{T_a(x), T_a(y)}(T_a(z)) = F^2_{x,y}(z),$$

$$\forall \beta \in \mathbb{R} : F^2_{R_\beta(x), R_\beta(y)}(R_\beta(z)) = F^2_{x,y}(z),$$

$$\forall \gamma \in (0, \infty) : F^2_{S_\gamma(x), S_\gamma(y)}(S_\gamma(z)) = F^2_{x,y}(z).$$

Proof:

$$F^2_{T_a(x), T_a(y)}(T_a(z)) = \frac{(z+a) - (x+a)}{(y+a) - (x+a)} = \frac{z-x}{y-x} = F^2_{x,y}(z)$$

$$F^2_{R_\beta(x), R_\beta(y)}(R_\beta(z)) = \frac{e^{i\beta}z - e^{i\beta}x}{e^{i\beta}y - e^{i\beta}x} = \frac{z-x}{y-x}$$

$$F^2_{S_\gamma(x), S_\gamma(y)}(S_\gamma(z)) = \frac{\gamma z - \gamma x}{\gamma y - \gamma x} = \frac{z-x}{y-x}$$

$\square$

Definition 3.4 The set of edges E is defined as follows:

$$E = \left\{ e \in \prod_{i \in \{1,2\}} \mathbb{R}^2 \;\middle|\; e_1 \neq e_2 \right\}$$

3.3. COMBINATIONS OF EDGES

Definition 3.5 *For $e^1 \in E$ the function $F^3_{e^1}$ is defined as follows:*

$$F^3_{e^1} : \begin{cases} E \to \mathbb{R}^4 \\ e^2 \mapsto \begin{pmatrix} \left(F^2_{e^1_1, e^1_2}(e^2_1)\right)_1 \\ \left(F^2_{e^1_1, e^1_2}(e^2_1)\right)_2 \\ \left(F^2_{e^1_1, e^1_2}(e^2_2)\right)_1 \\ \left(F^2_{e^1_1, e^1_2}(e^2_2)\right)_2 \end{pmatrix} \end{cases}$$

Definition 3.6 *For $a \in \mathbb{R}^2, \beta \in \mathbb{R}, \gamma \in (0, \infty)$ translation ET_a, rotation ER_β, scaling ES_γ of an edge are defined as follows:*

$$ET_a : \begin{cases} E \to E \\ e \mapsto \begin{pmatrix} T_a(e_1) \\ T_a(e_2) \end{pmatrix} \end{cases}$$

$$ER_\beta : \begin{cases} E \to E \\ e \mapsto \begin{pmatrix} R_\beta(e_1) \\ R_\beta(e_2) \end{pmatrix} \end{cases}$$

$$ES_\gamma : \begin{cases} E \to E \\ e \mapsto \begin{pmatrix} S_\gamma(e_1) \\ S_\gamma(e_2) \end{pmatrix} \end{cases}$$

Definition 3.7 *For the set of combinations C is defined as*

$$C = \bigcup_{m \in \mathbb{N}} E^{\{0,\dots,m\}}.$$

Definition 3.8 *For $a \in \mathbb{R}^2, \beta \in \mathbb{R}, \gamma \in (0, \infty)$ and translation CT_a, rotation CR_β, scaling CS_γ of a combination are defined as follows:*

$$CT_a : \begin{cases} C \to C \\ c \mapsto (ET_a(e_i))_{i \in \{0,\dots,m\}} \end{cases}$$

$$CR_\beta : \begin{cases} C \to C \\ c \mapsto (ER_\beta(e_i))_{i \in \{0,\dots,m\}} \end{cases}$$

$$CS_\gamma : \begin{cases} C \to C \\ c \mapsto (ES_\gamma(e_i))_{i \in \{0,\dots,m\}} \end{cases}$$

Definition 3.9

$$F^4 : \begin{cases} C \to \bigcup_{m \in \mathbb{N}} \mathbb{R}^{4m} \\ c \mapsto \left(F^3_{\infty}(c_i)\right)_{i \in \{1,\ldots,m\}} \end{cases}$$

Lemma 3.3 *For $a \in \mathbb{R}^2, \beta \in \mathbb{R}, \gamma \in (0, \infty)$ we get*

$$c \in C \implies \begin{cases} F^4(c) = F^4(CT_a(c)) \\ F^4(c) = F^4(CR_\beta(c)) \\ F^4(c) = F^4(CS_\gamma(c)) \end{cases} .$$

Definition 3.10 *The half metric d is defined as follows:*

$$d : \begin{cases} \bigcup_{m \in \mathbb{N}} E^{\{0,\ldots,m\}} \times E^{\{0,\ldots,m\}} \to \mathbb{R} \\ (c_1, c_2) \mapsto \|F^4(c_1) - F^4(c_2)\|_{\max} \end{cases}$$

Finally, a trivial object recognition system invariant to rotation, translation and scaling will be implemented now.

Task 3.1 *Assume $K \in \mathbb{N}, \varepsilon > 0$ and a sequence of combinations $c \in C^K$. Each combination $(e^k_i)_{i \in \{0,\ldots,l_k\}}$ has l_k+1 edges with $l_k \in \mathbb{N}$. Let $X \in E$ denote a finite set of edges extracted from an image to analyze. For each learned combination $(e^k_i)_{i \in \{0,\ldots,l_k\}}$ consider maximal $m_k \in \mathbb{N}$ for which a subsequence $\pi : \{0,\ldots,m_k\} \to \{0,\ldots,l_k\}$ with $\pi(0) = 0$ and a combination of extracted edges $\tilde{c} = (\tilde{e}_{i \in \{1,\ldots,m_k\}}) \subseteq X$ exist with*

$$d\left(\left(e^k_{\pi(i)}\right)_{i \in \{0,\ldots,m_k\}}, \tilde{c}\right) \leq \varepsilon. \tag{3.5}$$

For $M = \max_{k \in \{1,\ldots,K\}} m_k$ determine the set

$$I = \{k \in \{1,\ldots,K\} | m_k = M\}. \tag{3.6}$$

The algorithm should be denoted as $A^3_{\varepsilon,c}$.

Implementation: To implement the task the algorithm A^2 should be used. At first a sequence of feature vectors $(c_k)_{k \in \{1,\ldots,K\}}$ with $c_k \in \prod_{i \in \{1,\ldots,l_k\}} \mathbb{R}^4$ defined as $c_k = F^4(e^k)$ should be produced. After having built the storage for $A^2_{\varepsilon,c}$ from $(c_k)_{k \in \{1,\ldots,K\}}$ find $A^2_{\varepsilon,c}(X_e) = (M_e, I_e)$ with $X_e = \{F^4_e(\tilde{e}) | \tilde{e} \in X\}$ for each $e \in X$. For $M = \max_{e \in X} M_e$ the required set can be obtained as

$$I = \bigcup_{M_e = M} I_e. \tag{3.7}$$

$\square$

3.3. COMBINATIONS OF EDGES

3.3.2 Reflection Invariance

This section introduces a way to represent an edge combination invariantly to reflection in addition to rotation, scaling, translation. Different from the previous subsection the representation consists of two feature vectors: the old one for rotation, scaling, translation and the new one for reflection relative to an arbitrary axis. Again a simple object recognition system based on this representation will be introduced at the end of the subsection.

Definition 3.11 *For $\beta \in \mathbb{R}$ mirror reflection M_β is defined as follows:*

$$M_\beta : \begin{cases} \mathbb{R}^2 \to \mathbb{R}^2 \\ x \mapsto \begin{pmatrix} \cos\beta & \sin\beta \\ \sin\beta & -\cos\beta \end{pmatrix} \begin{pmatrix} x_1 \\ x_2 \end{pmatrix} \end{cases}$$

Lemma 3.4 *For $x, y \in \mathbb{R}^2, x \neq 0$ we have*

$$\forall \beta \in \mathbb{R} : F^1_{M_\beta(x)}(M_\beta(y)) = \begin{pmatrix} 1 & 0 \\ 0 & -1 \end{pmatrix} F^1_x(y).$$

Proof: As

$$\begin{pmatrix} 0 & -1 \\ 1 & 0 \end{pmatrix} \begin{pmatrix} \cos\beta & \sin\beta \\ \sin\beta & -\cos\beta \end{pmatrix} = -\begin{pmatrix} \cos\beta & \sin\beta \\ \sin\beta & -\cos\beta \end{pmatrix} \begin{pmatrix} 0 & -1 \\ 1 & 0 \end{pmatrix}$$

and

$$M_\beta M_\beta = \begin{pmatrix} 1 & 0 \\ 0 & 1 \end{pmatrix}$$

we get

$$F^1_{M_\beta(x)}(M_\beta(y)) = \frac{1}{M_\beta(x)_1^2 + M_\beta(x)_2^2} \begin{pmatrix} M_\beta(x)_1 & M_\beta(x)_2 \\ -M_\beta(x)_2 & M_\beta(x)_1 \end{pmatrix} \begin{pmatrix} M_\beta(y)_1 \\ M_\beta(y)_2 \end{pmatrix}$$

$$= \frac{1}{<M_\beta(x), M_\beta(x)>} \begin{pmatrix} <M_\beta(x), M_\beta(y)> \\ \left\langle \begin{pmatrix} 0 & -1 \\ 1 & 0 \end{pmatrix} M_\beta(x), M_\beta(y) \right\rangle \end{pmatrix}$$

$$= \frac{1}{<M_\beta(x), M_\beta(x)>} \begin{pmatrix} <M_\beta(x), M_\beta(y)> \\ -\left\langle M_\beta \begin{pmatrix} 0 & -1 \\ 1 & 0 \end{pmatrix} x, M_\beta(y) \right\rangle \end{pmatrix}$$

$$= \frac{1}{<x, x>} \begin{pmatrix} <x, y> \\ -\left\langle \begin{pmatrix} 0 & -1 \\ 1 & 0 \end{pmatrix} x, y \right\rangle \end{pmatrix} = \begin{pmatrix} 1 & 0 \\ 0 & -1 \end{pmatrix} F^1_x(y).$$

Corollary 3.1 *For $x, y, z \in \mathbb{R}^2, x \neq y$ we have*

$$\forall \beta \in \mathbb{R} : F^2_{M_\beta(x), M_\beta(y)}(M_\beta(z)) = \begin{pmatrix} 1 & 0 \\ 0 & -1 \end{pmatrix} F^2_{x,y}(z).$$

Definition 3.12 *For $\beta \in \mathbb{R}$ edge mirroring EM_β is defined as follows:*

$$EM_\beta : \begin{cases} E \to E \\ e \mapsto \begin{pmatrix} M_\beta(e_1) \\ M_\beta(e_2) \end{pmatrix} \end{cases}$$

Definition 3.13 *For $\beta \in \mathbb{R}$ combination mirroring CM_β^m is defined as follows:*

$$CM_\beta : \begin{cases} C \to C \\ c \mapsto (EM_\beta(c_i))_{i \in \{0, \ldots, m\}} \end{cases}$$

Lemma 3.5 *For $c \in C_m$ we get*

$$\forall \beta \in \mathbb{R} : F^4(CM_\beta(c)) = F^4(CM_0(c)).$$

Now, a trivial object recognition system invariant to rotation, translation, scaling and rotation will be implemented.

Task 3.2 *Assume $K \in \mathbb{N}, \varepsilon > 0$ and a sequence of combinations $c \in C^K$. Each combination $(e_i^k)_{i \in \{0, \ldots, l_k\}}$ has $l_k + 1$ edges with $l_k \in \mathbb{N}$. Let $X \in E$ denote a finite set of edges extracted from an image to analyze. For each learned combination $(e_i^k)_{i \in \{0, \ldots, l_k\}}$ consider maximal $m_k \in \mathbb{N}$ for which a subsequence $\pi : \{0, \ldots, m_k\} \to \{0, \ldots, l_k\}$ with $\pi(0) = 0$ and a combination of extracted edges $\check{c} = (\check{e}_{i \in \{1, \ldots, m_k\}}) \subseteq X$ exist with*

$$\begin{gathered} d\left(\left(e^k_{\pi(i)}\right)_{i \in \{0, \ldots, m_k\}}, \check{c}\right) \leq \varepsilon \\ \vee \\ d\left(\left(e^k_{\pi(i)}\right)_{i \in \{0, \ldots, m_k\}}, CM_0(\check{c})\right) \leq \varepsilon \end{gathered} \quad (3.8)$$

For $M = \max_{k \in \{1, \ldots, K\}} m_k$ determine the set

$$I = \{k \in \{1, \ldots, K\} | m_k = M\}. \quad (3.9)$$

The algorithm should be denoted as $A^4_{\varepsilon, c}$.

3.3. COMBINATIONS OF EDGES

Implementation: For
$$\tilde{c} \in \prod_{k \in \{1,...,2K\}} C$$
with
$$k \in \{1, ..., K\} \Rightarrow \tilde{c}_{2k-1} = c_k, \tilde{c}_{2k} = CM_0(c_k)$$
build $A^3_{\varepsilon,\tilde{c}}$ as in Task 3.1. Finally build the algorithm as follows:
$$A^4_{\varepsilon,c}(X) = \left\{ \left\lceil \frac{k}{2} \right\rceil \middle| k \in A^3_{\varepsilon,\tilde{c}}(X) \right\}$$

□

3.3.3 Projection Robustness

Basically this subsection shows how to build a net shown in the Figure 3.4 and denoted as $N^C_{\varepsilon,\gamma}$ later on. The object recognition system constructed subsequently stores several variants of the object representation transformed with respect to each cell. It makes the system robust to perspective change.

Definition 3.14 *For $(\alpha, \beta) \in (0, \pi) \times \mathbb{R}$ inclination I_α and projection $P_{\alpha,\beta}$ are defined as follows:*

$$I_\alpha : \begin{cases} \mathbb{R}^2 \to \mathbb{R}^2 \\ x \mapsto \begin{pmatrix} \sin \alpha & 0 \\ 0 & 1 \end{pmatrix} \begin{pmatrix} x_1 \\ x_2 \end{pmatrix} \end{cases}$$

$$P_{\alpha,\beta} : \begin{cases} \mathbb{R}^2 \to \mathbb{R}^2 \\ x \mapsto I_\alpha \circ R_\beta(x) \end{cases}$$

Definition 3.15 *For $x, y \in \mathbb{R}^2, x \neq 0$ the function $F^5_{x,y}$ is defined as follows:*

$$F^5_{x,y} : \begin{cases} (0, \pi) \times \mathbb{R} \to \mathbb{R}^2 \\ (\alpha, \beta) \mapsto F^1_{P_{\alpha,\beta}(x)}(P_{\alpha,\beta}(y)) \end{cases}$$

Lemma 3.6 *For $x \in \mathbb{R}^2$ and $(\alpha, \beta) \in (0, \pi) \times \mathbb{R}$ exists $\gamma_x \in \mathbb{R}$ with*

$$P_{\alpha,\beta}(x) = \|x\| \begin{pmatrix} \sin \alpha \cos(\gamma_x + \beta) \\ \sin(\gamma_x + \beta) \end{pmatrix}.$$

Proof: For $\gamma_x \in \mathbb{R}$ with

$$x = \|x\| \begin{pmatrix} \cos \gamma_x \\ \sin \gamma_x \end{pmatrix}$$

we get

$$P_{\alpha,\beta}(x) = I_\alpha \left(\|x\| \begin{pmatrix} \cos \beta & -\sin \beta \\ \sin \beta & \cos \beta \end{pmatrix} \begin{pmatrix} \cos \gamma_x \\ \sin \gamma_x \end{pmatrix} \right)$$

$$= \|x\| \begin{pmatrix} \sin \alpha & 0 \\ 0 & 1 \end{pmatrix} \begin{pmatrix} \cos(\gamma_x + \beta) \\ \sin(\gamma_x + \beta) \end{pmatrix}.$$

□

3.3. COMBINATIONS OF EDGES

Corollary 3.2 *For $x \in \mathbb{R}^2 \setminus \{0\}, y \in \mathbb{R}^2$ exist $\gamma_x, \gamma_y \in \mathbb{R}$ with*

$$\forall (\alpha, \beta) \in (0, \pi) \times \mathbb{R}:$$

$$F_{x,y}^5(\alpha, \beta) = \frac{\|y\|}{\|x\|} \begin{pmatrix} \frac{\sin^2\alpha \cos(\gamma_x+\beta)\cos(\gamma_y+\beta) + \sin(\gamma_x+\beta)\sin(\gamma_y+\beta)}{\sin^2\alpha \cos^2(\gamma_x+\beta) + \sin^2(\gamma_x+\beta)} \\ \frac{\sin\alpha \sin(\gamma_y - \gamma_x)}{\sin^2\alpha \cos^2(\gamma_x+\beta) + \sin^2(\gamma_x+\beta)} \end{pmatrix}.$$

Lemma 3.7 *For $x \in \mathbb{R}^2 \setminus \{0\}, y \in \mathbb{R}^2$ we have*

$$\forall (\alpha, \beta) \in (0, \pi) \times \mathbb{R}: \|\partial_\alpha F_{x,y}^5(\alpha, \beta)\|_{\max}, \|\partial_\beta F_{x,y}^5(\alpha, \beta)\|_{\max} \leq \frac{\|y\|}{\|x\|} \cdot \frac{2}{\sin^4 \alpha}.$$

Proof: At first set

$$a = \begin{pmatrix} \cos(\gamma_x + \beta) \\ \sin(\gamma_x + \beta) \end{pmatrix}, b = \begin{pmatrix} \cos(\gamma_y + \beta) \\ \sin(\gamma_y + \beta) \end{pmatrix}.$$

Then we get

$$\partial_\alpha \left(\frac{\sin^2\alpha \cos(\gamma_x+\beta)\cos(\gamma_y+\beta) + \sin(\gamma_x+\beta)\sin(\gamma_y+\beta)}{\sin^2\alpha \cos^2(\gamma_x+\beta) + \sin^2(\gamma_x+\beta)} \right) = \partial_\alpha \left(\frac{a_1 b_1 \sin^2\alpha + a_2 b_2}{a_1^2 \sin^2\alpha + a_2^2} \right)$$

$$= \frac{2 a_1 b_1 \sin\alpha \cos\alpha (a_1^2 \sin^2\alpha + a_2^2) - 2 a_1^2 \sin\alpha \cos\alpha (a_1 b_1 \sin^2\alpha + a_2 b_2)}{(a_1^2 \sin^2\alpha + a_2^2)^2}$$

$$= \frac{a_1 a_2 \sin 2\alpha (b_1 a_2 - a_1 b_2)}{(a_1^2 \sin^2\alpha + a_2^2)^2}.$$

As

$$b_1 a_2 - a_1 b_2 = \cos(\gamma_y + \beta)\sin(\gamma_x + \beta) - \cos(\gamma_x + \beta)\sin(\gamma_y + \beta) = \sin(\gamma_x - \gamma_y)$$

we get

$$|(\partial_\alpha F_{x,y}^5(\alpha, \beta))_1| = \left| \frac{\|y\|}{\|x\|} \cdot \frac{\cos(\gamma_x+\beta)\sin(\gamma_x+\beta)\sin 2\alpha \sin(\gamma_x-\gamma_y)}{(\sin^2\alpha \cos^2(\gamma_x+\beta) + \sin^2(\gamma_x+\beta))^2} \right| \leq \frac{\|y\|}{\|x\|} \cdot \frac{1}{\sin^4 \alpha}.$$

As

$$\partial_\alpha \frac{\sin\alpha}{\sin^2\alpha \cos^2(\gamma_x+\beta) + \sin^2(\gamma_x+\beta)} = \partial_\alpha \frac{\sin\alpha}{a_1^2 \sin^2\alpha + a_2^2}$$

$$= \frac{\cos\alpha (a_1^2 \sin^2\alpha + a_2^2) - 2 a_1^2 \sin\alpha \cos\alpha \sin\alpha}{(a_1^2 \sin^2\alpha + a_2^2)^2} = \frac{a_2^2 \cos\alpha - a_1^2 \sin^2\alpha \cos\alpha}{(a_1^2 \sin^2\alpha + a_2^2)^2}$$

we get

$$|(\partial_\alpha F_{x,y}^5(\alpha, \beta))_2| = \left| \partial_\alpha \left(\frac{\|y\|}{\|x\|} \cdot \frac{\sin\alpha \sin(\gamma_y - \gamma_x)}{\sin^2\alpha \cos^2(\gamma_x+\beta) + \sin^2(\gamma_x+\beta)} \right) \right|$$

$$= \left|\frac{\|y\|}{\|x\|} \cdot \frac{(a_2^2 \cos\alpha - a_1^2 \sin^2\alpha \cos\alpha)\sin(\gamma_y - \gamma_x)}{(a_1^2 \sin^2\alpha + a_2^2)^2}\right|$$

$$\leq \frac{\|y\|}{\|x\|} \cdot \frac{a_2^2 + a_1^2}{(a_1^2 \sin^2\alpha + a_2^2 \sin^2\alpha)^2} = \frac{\|y\|}{\|x\|} \cdot \frac{1}{\sin^4\alpha}$$

$$|(\partial_\beta F_{x,y}^5(\alpha,\beta))_1| \leq \frac{\|y\|}{\|x\|} \cdot \frac{2}{\sin^4\alpha}.$$

As

$$\partial_\beta \left(\frac{1}{\sin^2\alpha\cos^2(\gamma_x+\beta) + \sin^2(\gamma_x+\beta)}\right) = \frac{-\cos^2\alpha\sin(2(\gamma_x+\beta))}{(\sin^2\alpha\cos^2(\gamma_x+\beta) + \sin^2(\gamma_x+\beta))^2}$$

we get

$$|(\partial_\beta F_{x,y}^5(\alpha,\beta))_2| = \left|\partial_\beta\left(\frac{\|y\|}{\|x\|} \cdot \frac{\sin\alpha\sin(\gamma_y - \gamma_x)}{\sin^2\alpha\cos^2(\gamma_x+\beta) + \sin^2(\gamma_x+\beta)}\right)\right|$$

$$\leq \frac{\|y\|}{\|x\|} \cdot \frac{1}{\sin^4\alpha}.$$

□

Corollary 3.3 *For $x \in \mathbb{R}^2 \setminus \{0\}, y \in \mathbb{R}^2$ we have*

$$\forall \alpha, \alpha' \in (0,\pi) \forall \beta, \beta' \in \mathbb{R} \forall \delta > 0, \alpha + \delta < \pi:$$

$$|\alpha - \alpha'|, |\beta - \beta'| \leq \delta \Rightarrow \|F_{x,y}^5(\alpha,\beta) - F_{x,y}^5(\alpha',\beta')\|_{\max} \leq \frac{\|y\|}{\|x\|} \cdot \frac{4\delta}{\sin^4(\alpha+\delta)}.$$

Proof: As for some $\tilde\alpha_{1/2} \in (\alpha,\alpha'), \tilde\beta_{1/2} \in (\beta,\beta')$ we have

$$|(F_{x,y}^5(\alpha,\beta))_{1/2} - (F_{x,y}^5(\alpha',\beta))_{1/2}| = |\partial_\alpha F_{x,y}^5(\tilde\alpha_{1/2},\beta)(\alpha-\alpha')| \leq \frac{\|y\|}{\|x\|} \cdot \frac{2\delta}{\sin^4(\alpha+\delta)}$$

and

$$|(F_{x,y}^5(\alpha',\beta))_{1/2} - (F_{x,y}^5(\alpha',\beta'))_{1/2}| = |\partial_\beta F_{x,y}^5(\alpha',\tilde\beta_{1/2})(\beta-\beta')| \leq \frac{\|y\|}{\|x\|} \cdot \frac{2\delta}{\sin^4(\alpha+\delta)}$$

we get

$$\|F_{x,y}^5(\alpha,\beta) - F_{x,y}^5(\alpha',\beta')\|_{\max} \leq$$
$$\|F_{x,y}^5(\alpha,\beta) - F_{x,y}^5(\alpha',\beta)\|_{\max} + \|F_{x,y}^5(\alpha',\beta) - F_{x,y}^5(\alpha',\beta')\|_{\max}$$
$$\leq \frac{\|y\|}{\|x\|} \cdot \frac{4\delta}{\sin^4(\alpha+\delta)}.$$

□

The following definition of the net $N_{\varepsilon,\gamma}^C$ has plays a very important role for the construction of an object recognition system robust to perspective change. The net describes how to chose the red points from the Figure 3.4.

3.3. COMBINATIONS OF EDGES

Definition 3.16 *For $\varepsilon, C > 0$ observe the sequences $(\alpha_n)_{n \in \mathbb{N}_0}$ and $(\delta_n)_{n \in \mathbb{N}_0}$ defined as follows:*

$$n = 0 : \begin{cases} \alpha_n = \pi/2 \\ \delta_n = \sup\left\{\delta > 0 \,\Big|\, C \cdot \frac{4\delta}{\sin^4(\alpha_n + \delta)} \leq \varepsilon, \alpha_n + \delta < \pi \right\} \end{cases}$$

$$n \in \mathbb{N} : \begin{cases} \delta_n = \sup\left\{\delta > 0 \,\Big|\, C \cdot \frac{4\delta}{\sin^4(\alpha_{n-1} + \delta_{n-1} + 2\delta)} \leq \varepsilon, \alpha_{n-1} + \delta_{n-1} + 2\delta < \pi \right\} \\ \alpha_n = \alpha_{n-1} + \delta_{n-1} + \delta_n \end{cases}$$

For

$$M = \left(\left\lceil \frac{\pi}{\delta_n} \right\rceil\right)_{n \in \mathbb{N}_0}$$

and $n \in \mathbb{N}_0$ observe the sequence $\beta^n \in \mathbb{R}^{\{1,\ldots,M_n\}}$ defined as follows:

$$\beta^n = (2(m-1)\delta_n + \delta_n)_{m \in \{1,\ldots,M_n\}}$$

For

$$\gamma \in [0, \pi/2), \quad N = \inf\{n \in \mathbb{N}_0 | \alpha_n + \delta_n \geq \pi/2 + \gamma\}$$

the net $N^C_{\varepsilon, \gamma}$ is defined as follows:

$$N^C_{\varepsilon, \gamma} = (\alpha_n, (\beta^n_m)_{m \in \{1,\ldots,M_n\}})_{n \in \{0,\ldots,N\}}$$

Lemma 3.8 *For $\varepsilon, C > 0$ set $(\alpha_n)_{n \in \mathbb{N}_0}$ as above, then*

$$\forall \gamma \in [0, \pi/2) \, \exists n \in \mathbb{N}_0 : \alpha_n + \delta_n \geq \pi/2 + \gamma.$$

Proof by contradiction: Let us assume that

$$\exists \gamma \in [0, \pi/2) \, \forall n \in \mathbb{N}_0 : \alpha_n + \delta_n < \pi/2 + \gamma.$$

Obviously we have

$$\forall n \in \mathbb{N} : C \cdot \frac{4\delta_n}{\sin^4(\alpha_n + \delta_n)} = \varepsilon.$$

Set

$$\tilde{\delta} = \frac{\varepsilon \sin^4(\pi/2 + \gamma)}{4C}.$$

Direct consequence is

$$C \cdot \frac{4\tilde{\delta}}{\sin^4(\pi/2 + \gamma)} = \varepsilon.$$

As
$$\forall n \in \mathbb{N} : \sin^4(\alpha_n + \delta_n) > \sin^4(\pi/2 + \gamma)$$
we immediately get
$$\forall n \in \mathbb{N} : \tilde{\delta} < \delta_n.$$
As
$$\forall n \in \mathbb{N} : \alpha_n + \delta_n = \pi/2 + \delta_0 + \sum_{i=1}^{n} 2\delta_i \geq \pi/2 + \delta_0 + 2n\tilde{\delta}$$
we get a contradiction. □

Lemma 3.9 *For $\varepsilon, C > 0, \gamma \in [0, \pi/2)$ build the net*
$$N_{\varepsilon,\gamma}^{C} = (\alpha_n, (\beta_m^n)_{m \in \{1,...,M_n\}})_{n \in \{0,...,N\}}.$$
Then for $x \in \mathbb{R}^2 \setminus \{0\}, y \in \mathbb{R}^2$ with $\frac{\|y\|}{\|x\|} \leq C$ we get
$$\forall (\alpha, \beta) \in [\pi/2, \pi/2 + \gamma] \times \mathbb{R} \; \exists (n, m) \in \{0,...,N\} \times \{1,...,M_n\} :$$
$$\|F_{x,y}^5(\alpha, \beta) - F_{x,y}^5(\alpha_n, \beta_m^n)\|_{\max} \leq \varepsilon.$$

Proof: For $\tilde{\beta} \in [0, 2\pi]$ with
$$\exists n \in \mathbb{Z} : \tilde{\beta} + 2n\pi = \beta$$
we get by construction of $N_{\varepsilon,\gamma}^{C}$ that
$$\exists (n, m) \in \{0,...,N\} \times \{1,...,M_n\} : |\alpha - \alpha_n|, |\tilde{\beta} - \beta_m^n| \leq \delta_n.$$
Finally
$$\|F_{x,y}^5(\alpha, \beta) - F_{x,y}^5(\alpha_n, \beta_m^n)\|_{\max} = \|F_{x,y}^5(\alpha, \tilde{\beta}) - F_{x,y}^5(\alpha_n, \beta_m^n)\|_{\max}$$
$$\leq \frac{\|y\|}{\|x\|} \cdot \frac{4\delta_n}{\sin^4(\alpha_n + \delta_n)} \leq C \cdot \frac{4\delta_n}{\sin^4(\alpha_n + \delta_n)} \leq \varepsilon.$$
□

Lemma 3.10 *For $\alpha \in (0, \pi), \beta \in \mathbb{R}$ and $x \in \mathbb{R}^2 \setminus \{0\}, y \in \mathbb{R}^2$ we have*
$$F_{x,y}^5(\pi - \alpha, \beta + \pi) = F_{x,y}^5(\alpha, \pi).$$

3.3. COMBINATIONS OF EDGES

Proof: As

$$P_{\pi-\alpha,\beta+\pi} = \begin{pmatrix} \sin(\pi-\alpha) & 0 \\ 0 & 1 \end{pmatrix} \begin{pmatrix} \cos(\beta+\pi) & -\sin(\beta+\pi) \\ \sin(\beta+\pi) & \cos(\beta+\pi) \end{pmatrix}$$

$$= \begin{pmatrix} \sin\alpha & 0 \\ 0 & 1 \end{pmatrix} \begin{pmatrix} -\cos\beta & \sin\beta \\ -\sin\beta & -\cos\beta \end{pmatrix} = -P_{\alpha,\beta}$$

we get

$$F^1_{P_{\pi-\alpha,\beta+\pi}(x)}(P_{\pi-\alpha,\beta+\pi}(y)) = F^1_{-P_{\alpha,\beta}(x)}(-P_{\alpha,\beta}(y)) = F^1_{P_{\alpha,\beta}(x)}(P_{\alpha,\beta}(y)).$$

□

Corollary 3.4 *For $\varepsilon, C > 0, \gamma \in [0, \pi/2)$ build the net*

$$N^C_{\varepsilon,\gamma} = (\alpha_n, (\beta^n_m)_{m \in \{1,...,M_n\}})_{n \in \{0,...,N\}}.$$

Then for $x \in \mathbb{R}^2\setminus\{0\}, y \in \mathbb{R}^2$ with $\frac{\|y\|}{\|x\|} \leq C$ we get

$$\forall (\alpha, \beta) \in [\pi/2 - \gamma, \pi/2] \times \mathbb{R} \; \exists (n, m) \in \{0, ..., N\} \times \{1, ..., M_n\} :$$

$$\|F^5_{x,y}(\alpha, \beta) - F^5_{x,y}(\alpha_n, \beta^n_m)\|_{\max} \leq \varepsilon.$$

Proof: As $\pi - \alpha \in [\pi/2, \pi/2 + \gamma]$

$$\exists (n, m) \in \{0, ..., N\} \times \{1, ..., M_n\} :$$

$$\varepsilon \geq \|F^5_{x,y}(\pi - \alpha, \beta + \pi) - F^5_{x,y}(\alpha_n, \beta^n_m)\|_{\max} = \|F^5_{x,y}(\alpha, \beta) - F^5_{x,y}(\alpha_n, \beta^n_m)\|_{\max}.$$

□

Lemma 3.11 *For $\varepsilon, C > 0, \gamma \in [0, \pi/2)$ build the net*

$$N^C_{\varepsilon,\gamma} = (\alpha_n, (\beta^n_m)_{m \in \{1,...,M_n\}})_{n \in \{0,...,N\}}.$$

Then for

$$(x, y), (u, v) \in \mathbb{R}^2\setminus\{0\} \times \mathbb{R}^2$$

with $\frac{\|y\|}{\|x\|} \leq C$ we have

$$\exists (\alpha, \beta) \in [\pi/2 - \gamma, \pi/2 + \gamma] \times \mathbb{R} : \|F^5_{x,y}(\alpha, \beta) - F^1_u(v)\|_{\max} \leq \delta \implies$$

$$\exists (n, m) \in \{0, ..., N\} \times \{1, ..., M_n\} : \|F^5_{x,y}(\alpha_n, \beta^n_m) - F^1_u(v)\|_{\max} \leq \delta + \varepsilon$$

with $\delta > 0$.

Proof: For $(n,m) \in \{0,...,N\} \times \{1,...,M_n\}$ with
$$\|F_{x,y}^5(\alpha,\beta) - F_{x,y}^5(\alpha_n,\beta_m^n)\|_{\max} \leq \varepsilon.$$
we get
$$\|F_{x,y}^5(\alpha_n,\beta_m^n) - F_u^1(v)\|_{\max} \leq$$
$$\|F_{x,y}^5(\alpha_n,\beta_m^n) - F_{x,y}^5(\alpha,\beta)\|_{\max} + \|F_{x,y}^5(\alpha,\beta) - F_u^1(v)\|_{\max} \leq \delta + \varepsilon$$
$\square$

Definition 3.17 For $L, \min > 0$ the set $E_{L,\min} \subseteq E$ is defined in the following way:
$$E_{L,\min} = \left\{ e \in \prod_{i \in \{1,2\}} [0,L]^2 \,\middle|\, \|e_2 - e_1\| \geq \min \right\}$$

Lemma 3.12 For $e \in E_{L,\min}$ and $a \in [0,L]^2$ set
$$x = e_2 - e_1, \ y = a - e_1.$$
Then we get
$$\frac{\|y\|}{\|x\|} \leq \frac{\sqrt{2}L}{\min}.$$

Definition 3.18 For $(\alpha,\beta) \in (0,\pi) \times \mathbb{R}$ edge projection $EP_{\alpha,\beta}$ is defined as follows:
$$EP_{\alpha,\beta} : \begin{cases} E \to E \\ e \mapsto \begin{pmatrix} P_{\alpha,\beta}(e_1) \\ P_{\alpha,\beta}(e_2) \end{pmatrix} \end{cases}$$

Definition 3.19 For $(\alpha,\beta) \in (0,\pi) \times \mathbb{R}$ combination projection $CP_{\alpha,\beta}$ is defined as follows:
$$CP_{\alpha,\beta} : \begin{cases} C \to C \\ c = (e_i)_{i \in \{0,...,m\}} \mapsto (EP_{\alpha,\beta}(e_i))_{i \in \{0,...,m\}} \end{cases}$$

Lemma 3.13 For $(\alpha,\beta,\gamma) \in (0,\pi) \times \mathbb{R} \times \mathbb{R}$ and $m \in \mathbb{N}$ we have
$$c \in C_m \Rightarrow CP_{\alpha,\beta} \circ CM_\gamma(c) = CP_{\alpha,\beta+\gamma} \circ CM_0(c).$$

3.3. COMBINATIONS OF EDGES

Proof: As
$$M_\gamma = R_\gamma \circ M_0$$
we get
$$P_{\alpha,\beta} \circ M_\gamma = I_\alpha \circ R_\beta \circ R_\gamma \circ M_0 = P_{\alpha,\beta+\gamma} \circ M_0.$$
□

At last, an object recognition system invariant to rotation, translation, scaling, reflection and robust to perspective change will be implemented.

Task 3.3 *Assume $K \in \mathbb{N}, \varepsilon > 0, \gamma \in [0, \pi/2)$ and a sequence of combinations $c \in C^K$. Each combination $(e_i^k)_{i \in \{0,...,l_k\}}$ has $l_k + 1$ edges with $l_k \in \mathbb{N}$. Let $X \in E$ denote a finite set of edges extracted from an image to analyze. For each learned combination $(e_i^k)_{i \in \{0,...,l_k\}}$ consider maximal $m_k \in \mathbb{N}$ for which a subsequence $\pi : \{0, ..., m_k\} \to \{0, ..., l_k\}$ with $\pi(0) = 0$, a combination of extracted edges $\tilde{c} = (\tilde{e}_{i \in \{1,...,m_k\}}) \subseteq X$ and $(\alpha, \beta) \in [\pi/2 - \gamma, \pi/2 + \gamma] \times \mathbb{R}$ exist with*

$$d\left(CP_{\alpha,\beta}\left(e_{\pi(i)}^k\right)_{i \in \{0,...,m_k\}}, \tilde{c}\right) \leq \varepsilon$$
$$\vee \qquad (3.10)$$
$$d\left(CP_{\alpha,\beta}\left(CM_0\left(e_{\pi(i)}^k\right)_{i \in \{0,...,m_k\}}\right), \tilde{c}\right) \leq \varepsilon$$

For $M = \max_{k \in \{1,...,K\}} m_k$ determine the set

$$I = \{k \in \{1, ..., K\} | m_k = M\}. \qquad (3.11)$$

The algorithm should be denoted as $A_{\varepsilon,c,\gamma}^5$.

Implementation: For $\delta > 0$ build the net
$$N_{\delta,\gamma}^{\min \frac{\sqrt{2}L}{}} = (\alpha_n, (\beta_m^n)_{m \in \{1,...,M_n\}})_{n \in \{0,...,N\}}$$
For $S = \sum_{n=0}^{N} M_n$ build the bijective function
$$g : \begin{cases} \bigcup_{n \in \{0,...,N\}} \{n\} \times \{1, ..., M_n\} \to \{1, ..., S\} \\ (n, m) \mapsto \sum_{i=0}^{n-1} M_n + m \end{cases}.$$
For the sequence $\tilde{c} \in C^{\{1,...,KS\}}$ defined as
$$\tilde{c}_i = c \Leftrightarrow \begin{cases} \exists k, s \in \{0, ..., K-1\} \times \{1, ..., S\} : \\ i = kS + s \wedge (n, m) = g^{-1}(s) \Rightarrow c = CP_{\alpha_n, \beta_m^n}(c_{k+1}) \end{cases}$$
build $A_{\varepsilon+\delta,\tilde{c}}^4$ as in Task 3.2. Finally build the approximation in the following way
$$A_{\varepsilon,c,\gamma}^5(X) = \left\{ \left\lceil \frac{k}{S} \right\rceil \;\middle|\; k \in A_{\varepsilon+\delta,\tilde{c}}^4(X) \right\}. \qquad (3.12)$$
□

Figure 3.16: Adaptability of half ellipses: clearly fewer half ellipses(left) than lines(right) are needed to approximate a form.

3.4 Combinations of Half Ellipses

This section mainly introduces half ellipses in Subsection 3.4.1 and construction of a net $N^C_{\varepsilon,\gamma}$ due to make the half ellipse based representation robust to perspective change in Subsection 3.4.5.

3.4.1 Definition and Parametrization of a Half Ellipse

Now the representation on the basis of straight lines will be generalized. A line will be replaced by a half ellipse. At first a straight line is a half ellipse itself. Additionally half ellipses can obviously approximate a circle or an ellipse in a more robust way than a chain of lines. In other words half ellipses show a clearly richer variety of forms Figure 3.17 and therefore greater adaptability Figure 3.16 as simple lines. As a result fewer features are needed to describe a form which allows to save storage and runtime. Other than matching approach [Low04] or flow estimator [LT81] a half ellipse based system does not need characteristic points where it can dock at. It is useful as a circle for example has no characteristic points. The new approach uses half ellipses instead of ellipses because the two end points are needed for the invariant representation of a combination of half ellipses: the first point of the half ellipse of a combination gets mapped on the point of origin, the second - on $(1,0)^T$.

The purpose of this section is to introduce a half ellipse and to prove Theorem 3.1. Figure 3.18 shows how the bow of a half ellipse can be represented uniquely according to Theorem 3.1. The representation code emerges from the point M in the right part of the image after minimal post processing.

3.4. COMBINATIONS OF HALF ELLIPSES

Figure 3.17: Variety of forms of half ellipses.

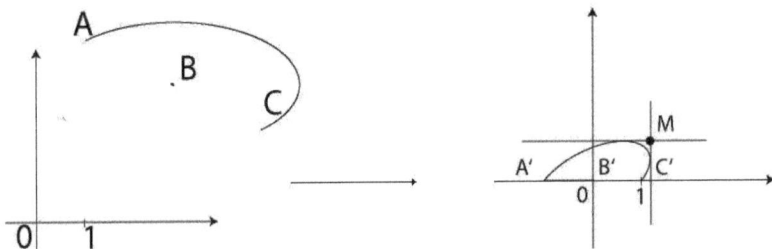

Figure 3.18: Representation of a half ellipse bow.

Definition 3.20 *The set of half ellipses HE is defined as follows:*

$$HE = \left\{ (e, B) \in E \times P(\mathbb{R}^2) \;\middle|\; \begin{array}{l} \exists (a, b, t_0, \delta) \in [0, \infty) \times [0, \infty) \times \mathbb{R} \times \{-1, 1\} \\ \exists (c, \beta, \gamma) \in \mathbb{R}^2 \times \mathbb{R} \times (0, \infty) : \\ B = \left\{ T_c \circ S_\gamma \circ R_\beta \begin{pmatrix} a\cos t \\ b\sin t \end{pmatrix} \;\middle|\; t \in \begin{array}{c} [t_0, t_0 + \delta\pi] \\ \cup \\ [t_0 + \delta\pi, t_0] \end{array} \right\}, \\ e_1 = T_c \circ S_\gamma \circ R_\beta \begin{pmatrix} a\cos t_0 \\ b\sin t_0 \end{pmatrix}, \\ e_2 = T_c \circ S_\gamma \circ R_\beta \begin{pmatrix} a\cos(t_0 + \pi) \\ b\sin(t_0 + \pi) \end{pmatrix} \end{array} \right\},$$

Definition 3.21 *The half ellipse producer HEP is defined as follows:*

$$HEP : \left\{ \begin{array}{l} ([0, \infty) \times (0, \infty) \cup (0, \infty) \times [0, \infty)) \times \mathbb{R} \times \{-1, 1\} \to HE \\ (a, b, t_0, \delta) \mapsto \left(\left(\begin{pmatrix} a\cos t_0 \\ b\sin t_0 \end{pmatrix}, \begin{pmatrix} a\cos(t_0 + \pi) \\ b\sin(t_0 + \pi) \end{pmatrix} \right), \left\{ \begin{pmatrix} a\cos t \\ b\sin t \end{pmatrix} \;\middle|\; t \in \begin{array}{c} [t_0, t_0 + \delta\pi] \\ \cup \\ [t_0 + \delta\pi, t_0] \end{array} \right\} \right) \end{array} \right.$$

Definition 3.22 *The function G^1 is defined as follows:*

$$G^1 : \begin{cases} HE \to \mathbb{R}^2 \\ (e,B) \mapsto \begin{pmatrix} \max_{x \in B} \left| \left(F^2_{\frac{e_1+e_2}{2},\, e_1}(x) \right)_1 \right| \\ \max_{x \in B} \left| \left(F^2_{\frac{e_1+e_2}{2},\, e_1}(x) \right)_2 \right| \end{pmatrix} \end{cases}$$

Definition 3.23 *The function G^2 is defined as follows:*

$$G^2 : \begin{cases} HE \to \mathbb{R}^2 \\ \left| \left(F^2_{\frac{e_1+e_2}{2},\, e_1}(x) \right)_1 \right| = G^1_1(e,B) \Rightarrow \\ G^2_1(e,B) = \left(F^2_{\frac{e_1+e_2}{2},\, e_1}(x) \right)_1 - SIGNUM\left(\left(F^2_{\frac{e_1+e_2}{2},\, e_1}(x) \right)_1 \right) \\ \left| \left(F^2_{\frac{e_1+e_2}{2},\, e_1}(x) \right)_2 \right| = G^1_2(e,B) \Rightarrow G^2_2(e,B) = \left(F^2_{\frac{e_1+e_2}{2},\, e_1}(x) \right)_2 \end{cases}$$

Lemma 3.14 *For*

$$(a,b,t_0,\delta) \in (0,\infty) \times (0,\infty) \times \mathbb{R} \times \{-1,1\},$$

$$(e,B) = HEP(a,b,t_0,\delta)$$

and

$$x : \begin{cases} \mathbb{R} \to \mathbb{C} \\ t \mapsto \begin{pmatrix} a\cos t \\ b\sin t \end{pmatrix} \end{cases}$$

we have

$$G^1_2(e,B) = \frac{ab}{\|x(t_0)\|^2}.$$

For $t_1 \in \mathbb{R}$ with $x(t_1) = i \cdot x(t_0) \cdot \frac{\|x(t_1)\|}{\|x(t_0)\|}$ we additionally get

$$G^1_1(e,B) = \frac{ab}{\|x(t_0)\|\|x(t_1)\|}.$$

Proof:

$$G^1_2(e,B) = \max_{t \in \mathbb{R}} \frac{ab|-\sin t_0 \cos t + \cos t_0 \sin t|}{a^2 \cos^2 t_0 + b^2 \sin^2 t_0}$$

3.4. COMBINATIONS OF HALF ELLIPSES

$$= \frac{ab|-\sin t_0 \cos(t_0 + \pi/2) + \cos t_0 \sin(t_0 + \pi/2)|}{\|x(t_0)\|^2}$$

$$= \frac{ab(\sin t_0 \sin t_0 + \cos t_0 \cos t_0)}{\|x(t_0)\|^2} = \frac{ab}{\|x(t_0)\|^2}.$$

For

$$y : \begin{cases} \mathbb{R} \to \mathbb{C} \\ t \mapsto \frac{x(t)}{x(t_0)} \end{cases}$$

and

$$z : \begin{cases} \mathbb{R} \to \mathbb{C} \\ t \mapsto \frac{x(t)}{x(t_1)} \end{cases}$$

we have

$$y(t) = \frac{x(t)}{x(t_0)} = \frac{x(t)}{x(t_1)} \cdot \frac{x(t_1)}{x(t_0)} = z(t) \cdot \frac{\|x(t_1)\|}{\|x(t_0)\|} \cdot i = (i\Re(z(t)) - \Im(z(t))) \frac{\|x(t_1)\|}{\|x(t_0)\|}.$$

For that reason

$$G_1^1(e, B) = \max_{t \in \mathbb{R}} |\Re(y(t))| = \max_{t \in \mathbb{R}} \left| \Im(z(t)) \frac{\|x(t_1)\|}{\|x(t_0)\|} \right|$$

$$= \max_{t \in \mathbb{R}} \frac{ab|-\sin t_1 \cos t + \cos t_1 \sin t|}{a^2 \cos^2 t_1 + b^2 \sin^2 t_1} \cdot \frac{\|x(t_1)\|}{\|x(t_0)\|} = \frac{ab}{\|x(t_0)\| \|x(t_1)\|}.$$

□

Definition 3.24 *For $\beta \in \mathbb{R}$ half ellipse rotation HER_β is defined as follows:*

$$HER_\beta : \begin{cases} HE \to HE \\ (e, B) \mapsto \left(\begin{pmatrix} R_\beta(e_1) \\ R_\beta(e_2) \end{pmatrix}, \{R_\beta(x) | x \in B\} \right) \end{cases}$$

Lemma 3.15 *For*

$$\left(\begin{pmatrix} a_1 \\ a_2 \end{pmatrix}, s \right) \in [0, \infty)^2 \times \mathbb{R}$$

with

$$\left\| \begin{pmatrix} a_1 \cos s \\ a_2 \sin s \end{pmatrix} \right\| = 1$$

assume

$$\left(\begin{pmatrix} a \\ b \end{pmatrix}, t_0 \right), \left(\begin{pmatrix} \tilde{a} \\ \tilde{b} \end{pmatrix}, \tilde{t}_0 \right) \in$$

$$\begin{cases} \left\{\begin{pmatrix} a_1 \\ a_2 \end{pmatrix}\right\} \times \\ \{s+2k\pi, -s+2k\pi, s+\pi+2k\pi, -s+\pi+2k\pi | k \in \mathbb{Z}\} \\ \cup \\ \left\{\begin{pmatrix} a_2 \\ a_1 \end{pmatrix}\right\} \times \\ \{s+\frac{\pi}{2}+2k\pi, -s-\frac{\pi}{2}+2k\pi, s+\frac{\pi}{2}+\pi+2k\pi, -s-\frac{\pi}{2}+\pi+2k\pi | k \in \mathbb{Z}\} \end{cases}$$

and
$$\delta, \tilde{\delta} \in \{-1, 1\}.$$

Then for
$$(e, B) = HEP(a, b, t_0, \delta), \ (\tilde{e}, \tilde{B}) = HEP(\tilde{a}, \tilde{b}, \tilde{t}_0, \tilde{\delta})$$

we get
$$G^2(e, B) = G^2(\tilde{e}, \tilde{B}) \Rightarrow \exists \beta \in \mathbb{R} : HER_\beta(e, B) = (\tilde{e}, \tilde{B}).$$

Lemma 3.16 *For*
$$(a, b, t_0, \delta), (\tilde{a}, \tilde{b}, \tilde{t}_0, \tilde{\delta}) \in [0, \infty) \times [0, \infty) \times \mathbb{R} \times \{-1, 1\}$$

with
$$\left\|\begin{pmatrix} a\cos t_0 \\ b\sin t_0 \end{pmatrix}\right\|, \left\|\begin{pmatrix} \tilde{a}\cos \tilde{t}_0 \\ \tilde{b}\sin \tilde{t}_0 \end{pmatrix}\right\| = 1$$

assume
$$(e, B) = HEP(a, b, t_0, \delta), \ (\tilde{e}, \tilde{B}) = HEP(\tilde{a}, \tilde{b}, \tilde{t}_0, \tilde{\delta}).$$

Then we get
$$G^2(e, B) = G^2(\tilde{e}, \tilde{B}) \Rightarrow \exists \beta \in \mathbb{R} : HER_\beta(e, B) = (\tilde{e}, \tilde{B}).$$

Proof: At first set
$$m = G^1(e, B).$$

As for $a = b$ or $ab = 0$ the statement is obvious assume
$$a \neq b, \ ab \neq 0.$$

For
$$x : \begin{cases} \mathbb{R} \to \mathbb{C} \\ t \mapsto \begin{pmatrix} a\cos t \\ b\sin t \end{pmatrix} \end{cases}$$

3.4. COMBINATIONS OF HALF ELLIPSES

choose $t_1 \in \mathbb{R}$ with
$$x(t_1) = i \cdot x(t_0) \cdot \|x(t_1)\|.$$

Considering
$$m_1 = \frac{ab}{\|x(t_1)\|}, \quad m_2 = ab$$

and

$$1 = \|x(t_0)\|^2 = a^2 \cos^2 t_0 + b^2 \sin^2 t_0 \Rightarrow \cos^2 t_0 = \frac{1-b^2}{a^2-b^2} \Rightarrow \cos^2 t_0 = \frac{a^2 - m_2^2}{a^4 - m_2^2}.$$

as well as

$$1 = \frac{x_1^2(t_1)}{a^2} + \frac{x_2^2(t_1)}{b^2} = \|x(t_1)\|^2 \left(\frac{b^2 \sin^2 t_0}{a^2} + \frac{a^2 \cos^2 t_0}{b^2} \right)$$

we get

$$b^4(1 - \cos^2 t_0) + a^4 \cos^2 t_0 = \frac{a^2 b^2}{\|x(t_1)\|^2} \Rightarrow b^4 + (a^4 - b^4) \cos^2 t_0 = m_1^2$$

$$\Rightarrow \frac{m_2^4}{a^4} + \left(a^4 - \frac{m_2^4}{a^4} \right) \left(\frac{a^2 - m_2^2}{a^4 - m_2^2} \right) = m_1^2 \Rightarrow a^2(a^4 - (m_1^2 + m_2^2)a^2 + m_2^2) = 0$$

$$\Rightarrow a_{1/2} = \sqrt{\frac{(m_1^2 + m_2^2) \pm \sqrt{(m_1^2 + m_2^2)^2 - 4m_2^2}}{2}}$$

$$\Rightarrow b_{1/2} = \frac{m_2}{a_{1/2}} = \sqrt{\frac{(m_1^2 + m_2^2) \mp \sqrt{(m_1^2 + m_2^2)^2 - 4m_2^2}}{2}} = a_{2/1}.$$

For $s \in \mathbb{R}$ with
$$\cos^2 s = \frac{1 - a_2^2}{a_1^2 - a_2^2}$$

we have

$$\frac{1 - a_1^2}{a_2^2 - a_1^2} = 1 - \frac{1 - a_2^2}{a_1^2 - a_2^2} = 1 - \cos^2 s = \sin^2 s = \cos^2(s + \pi/2).$$

For that reason
$$\left(\begin{pmatrix} a \\ b \end{pmatrix}, t_0 \right), \left(\begin{pmatrix} \tilde{a} \\ \tilde{b} \end{pmatrix}, \tilde{t}_0 \right) \in$$

$$\begin{cases} \left\{ \begin{pmatrix} a_1 \\ a_2 \end{pmatrix} \right\} \times \\ \{s + 2k\pi, -s + 2k\pi, s + \pi + 2k\pi, -s + \pi + 2k\pi | k \in \mathbb{Z}\} \\ \cup \\ \left\{ \begin{pmatrix} a_2 \\ a_1 \end{pmatrix} \right\} \times \\ \{s + \frac{\pi}{2} + 2k\pi, -s - \frac{\pi}{2} + 2k\pi, s + \frac{\pi}{2} + \pi + 2k\pi, -s - \frac{\pi}{2} + \pi + 2k\pi | k \in \mathbb{Z}\} \end{cases}.$$

$\square$

Lemma 3.17 *For $e \in E$ and*

$$(e, B_1), (e, B_2) \in HE$$

we have

$$G^2(e, B_1) = G^2(e, B_2) \Rightarrow B_1 = B_2.$$

Proof: It is known that

$$\exists (a_{1/2}, b_{1/2}, t_0^{1/2}, \delta_{1/2}) \in [0, \infty) \times [0, \infty) \times \mathbb{R} \times \{-1, 1\}$$

$$\exists (c_{1/2}, \alpha_{1/2}, \beta_{1/2}) \in \mathbb{R}^2 \times (0, \infty) \times \mathbb{R}:$$

$$B_{1/2} = \left\{ T_{c_{1/2}} \circ S_{\alpha_{1/2}} \circ R_{\beta_{1/2}} \begin{pmatrix} a_{1/2} \cos t \\ b_{1/2} \sin t \end{pmatrix} \middle| t \in \begin{matrix} [t_0^{1/2}, t_0^{1/2} + \delta_{1/2}\pi] \\ \cup \\ [t_0^{1/2} + \delta_{1/2}\pi, t_0^{1/2}] \end{matrix} \right\},$$

$$e_1 = T_{c_{1/2}} \circ S_{\alpha_{1/2}} \circ R_{\beta_{1/2}} \begin{pmatrix} a_{1/2} \cos t_0^{1/2} \\ b_{1/2} \sin t_0^{1/2} \end{pmatrix},$$

$$e_2 = T_{c_{1/2}} \circ S_{\alpha_{1/2}} \circ R_{\beta_{1/2}} \begin{pmatrix} a_{1/2} \cos(t_0^{1/2} + \pi) \\ b_{1/2} \sin(t_0^{1/2} + \pi) \end{pmatrix},$$

$$\left\| \begin{pmatrix} a_{1/2} \cos t_0^{1/2} \\ b_{1/2} \sin t_0^{1/2} \end{pmatrix} \right\| = 1.$$

As Lemma 3.16 shows

$$\exists \gamma \in \mathbb{R}: HER_\gamma(HEP(a_1, b_1, t_0^1, \delta_1)) = HEP(a_2, b_2, t_0^2, \delta_2).$$

For

$$x_{1/2}: \begin{cases} \mathbb{R} \to \mathbb{R}^2 \\ t \mapsto \begin{pmatrix} a_{1/2} \cos t \\ b_{1/2} \sin t \end{pmatrix} \end{cases}$$

3.4. COMBINATIONS OF HALF ELLIPSES

we get
$$\left\{T_{c_2} \circ S_{\alpha_2} \circ R_{\beta_2}(x_2(t)) \mid t \in [t_0^2, t_0^2 + \delta_2\pi] \cup [t_0^2 + \delta_2\pi, t_0^2]\right\}$$
$$= \left\{T_{c_2} \circ S_{\alpha_2} \circ R_{\beta_2} \circ R_\gamma(x_1(t)) \mid t \in [t_0^1, t_0^1 + \delta_1\pi] \cup [t_0^1 + \delta_1\pi, t_0^1]\right\}.$$

It remains to show
$$T_{c_2} \circ S_{\alpha_2} \circ R_{\beta_2} \circ R_\gamma = T_{c_1} \circ S_{\alpha_1} \circ R_{\beta_1}.$$

At first it will be shown
$$c_1 = c_2.$$

As for
$$x_1^1 = x_1(t_0^1), \; x_2^1 = x_1(t_0^1 + \delta_1\pi)$$

it is known
$$T_{c_2} \circ S_{\alpha_2} \circ R_{\beta_2} \circ R_\gamma(x_1^1) = e_1 = T_{c_1} \circ S_{\alpha_1} \circ R_{\beta_1}(x_1^1),$$
$$T_{c_2} \circ S_{\alpha_2} \circ R_{\beta_2} \circ R_\gamma(x_2^1) = e_2 = T_{c_1} \circ S_{\alpha_1} \circ R_{\beta_1}(x_2^1)$$

we get
$$0 = R_{\beta_1}(0) = R_{\beta_1}(x_1^1 + x_2^1) = R_{\beta_1}(x_1^1) + R_{\beta_1}(x_2^1)$$
$$= S_{\frac{1}{\alpha_1}} \circ T_{c_2 - c_1} \circ S_{\alpha_2} \circ R_{\beta_2} \circ R_\gamma(x_1^1) + S_{\frac{1}{\alpha_1}} \circ T_{c_2 - c_1} \circ S_{\alpha_2} \circ R_{\beta_2} \circ R_\gamma(x_2^1)$$
$$= S_{\frac{1}{\alpha_1}} \circ T_{2(c_2 - c_1)} \circ S_{\alpha_2} \circ R_{\beta_2} \circ R_\gamma(x_1^1 + x_2^1) = S_{\frac{1}{\alpha_1}} \circ T_{2(c_2 - c_1)}(0)$$
$$\Rightarrow T_{2(c_2 - c_1)}(0) = 0 \Rightarrow c_2 - c_1 = 0.$$

As $\|x_{1/2}(t_0^{1/2})\| = 1$ we automatically get $\alpha_1 = \alpha_2$. As $R_{\beta_1}(x_1^1) = R_{\beta_2 + \gamma}(x_1^1)$ we get $R_{\beta_1} = R_{\beta_2 + \gamma}$. □

Lemma 3.18 *For*
$$(a, b, t_0) \in [0, \infty) \times [0, \infty) \times \mathbb{R}$$

with
$$\left\| \begin{pmatrix} a \cos t_0 \\ b \sin t_0 \end{pmatrix} \right\| = 1$$

and
$$(e, B_1) = HEP(a, b, t_0, 1), \; (e, B_2) = HEP(a, b, t_0, -1)$$

we get
$$G_2^2(e, B_1) \geq 0, \; G_2^2(e, B_2) \leq 0 \text{ and } G_2^2(e, B_1) = -G_2^2(e, B_2).$$

Proof:
$$G_2^2(e, B_1) = \max_{t \in [t_0, t_0+\pi]} ab(-\sin t_0 \cos t + \cos t_0 \sin t)$$
$$= ab(-\sin t_0 \cos(t_0 + \pi/2) + \cos t_0 \sin(t_0 + \pi/2))$$
$$= ab(-\sin(-\pi/2)) = ab \sin(\pi/2) \geq 0$$
$$G_2^2(e, B_2) = \min_{t \in [t_0, t_0-\pi]} ab(-\sin t_0 \cos t + \cos t_0 \sin t)$$
$$= ab(-\sin t_0 \cos(t_0 - \pi/2) + \cos t_0 \sin(t_0 - \pi/2)) = ab(-\sin(\pi/2)) \leq 0$$
□

Lemma 3.19 *For*
$$(a, b, t_0, \delta) \in [0, \infty) \times [0, \infty) \times \mathbb{R} \times \{-1, 1\}$$
with
$$\left\| \begin{pmatrix} a \cos t_0 \\ b \sin t_0 \end{pmatrix} \right\| \neq 0$$
and
$$(e_1, B_1) = HEP(a, b, t_0, \delta), \quad (e_2, B_2) = HEP(a, b, -t_0, \delta)$$
we get
$$G_1^2(e_1, B_1) = -G_1^2(e_2, B_2).$$

Proof: Clair as for $s \in [0, \pi]$
$$a^2 \cos -t_0 \cos(-t_0 + \delta\pi - \delta s) + b^2 \sin -t_0 \sin(-t_0 + \delta\pi - \delta s)$$
$$= -(a^2 \cos t_0 \cos(t_0 + \delta s) + b^2 \sin t_0 \sin(t_0 + \delta s)).$$
□

Lemma 3.20
$$\forall x \in \mathbb{R}^2 \ \exists (e, B) \in HE : G^2(e, B) = x$$

Proof: For
$$m = \begin{pmatrix} |x_1| + 1 \\ |x_2| \end{pmatrix}$$
set
$$a = \sqrt{\frac{(m_1^2 + m_2^2) + \sqrt{(m_1^2 + m_2^2)^2 - 4m_2^2}}{2}},$$

3.4. COMBINATIONS OF HALF ELLIPSES

$$b = \sqrt{\frac{(m_1^2 + m_2^2) - \sqrt{(m_1^2 + m_2^2)^2 - 4m_2^2}}{2}}.$$

For $m = \begin{pmatrix} 1 \\ 1 \end{pmatrix}$ or $m_2 = 0$ the statement is obvious. Consider now

$$m \neq \begin{pmatrix} 1 \\ 1 \end{pmatrix} \Rightarrow a \neq b,$$

$$m_2 \neq 0 \Rightarrow b \neq 0.$$

Choose $t_0 \in \mathbb{R}$ with

$$\cos^2 t_0 = \frac{1 - b^2}{a^2 - b^2}.$$

Set

$$(e, B) = HEP(a, b, t_0, 1).$$

For

$$x : \begin{cases} \mathbb{R} \to \mathbb{R}^2 \\ t \mapsto \begin{pmatrix} a \cos t \\ b \sin t \end{pmatrix} \end{cases}$$

choose $t_1 \in \mathbb{R}$ in such a way that

$$x(t_1) = i \cdot x(t_0) \cdot \|x(t_1)\|.$$

As

$$G^1(e, B) = \begin{pmatrix} \frac{ab}{\|x(t_1)\|} \\ ab \end{pmatrix}$$

it must be shown now that

$$ab = m_2, \quad \|x(t_1)\| = \frac{m_2}{m_1}.$$

$$ab = \sqrt{\frac{(m_1^2 + m_2^2) + \sqrt{(m_1^2 + m_2^2)^2 - 4m_2^2}}{2}} \sqrt{\frac{(m_1^2 + m_2^2) - \sqrt{(m_1^2 + m_2^2)^2 - 4m_2^2}}{2}}$$

$$= \sqrt{\frac{(m_1^2 + m_2^2)^2 - (m_1^2 + m_2^2)^2 + 4m_2^2}{4}} = m_2$$

As

$$1 = \frac{x_1^2(t_1)}{a^2} + \frac{x_2^2(t_1)}{b^2} = \|x(t_1)\|^2 \left(\frac{b^2 \sin^2 t_0}{a^2} + \frac{a^2 \cos^2 t_0}{b^2} \right)$$

it remains to show that
$$\frac{b^2 \sin^2 t_0}{a^2} + \frac{a^2 \cos^2 t_0}{b^2} = \frac{m_1^2}{m_2^2}.$$
$$\frac{b^2 \sin^2 t_0}{a^2} + \frac{a^2 \cos^2 t_0}{b^2} = \frac{(a^2+b^2)-a^2b^2}{a^2b^2} = \frac{(m_1^2+m_2^2)-m_2^2}{m_2^2}$$

For
$$\delta : \begin{cases} \mathbb{R} \to \{-1, 1\} \\ x \mapsto -1\chi_{(-\infty,0)}(x) + \chi_{[0,\infty)}(x) \end{cases}$$

Lemma 3.18 shows that
$$x_2 = G_2^2(HEP(a, b, \pm t_0, \delta(x_2))).$$

If
$$x_1 = -G_1^2(HEP(a, b, t_0, \delta(x_2)))$$

Lemma 3.19 shows that
$$x_1 = G_1^2(HEP(a, b, -t_0, \delta(x_2))).$$

$\square$

Corollary 3.5
$$\forall e \in E, x \in \mathbb{R}^2 \; \exists (e, B) \in HE : G^2(e, B) = x$$

The following theorem is a typical existence and uniqueness statement. It says, for an edge $e \in E$ and a point $x \in \mathbb{R}^2$ there exists exactly one half ellipse (e, B) with e as endpoints and x a point encoding the bow of (e, B). The proof of the theorem results immediately from the previous considerations of the subsection.

Theorem 3.1
$$\forall e \in E, x \in \mathbb{R}^2 \; \exists^1 (e, B) \in HE : G^2(e, B) = x$$

Proof: Corollary 3.5 is directly the existence statement. Lemma 3.17 substantiates the uniqueness assertion.

$\square$

3.4.2 Invariance

This section is due to make some trivial statements requiring no proof. In a formal way it says, that the representation of a half ellipse bow showed above is invariant to rotation, translation, scaling.

Definition 3.25 *For $a \in \mathbb{R}^2, \beta \in \mathbb{R}, \gamma \in (0, \infty)$ translation HET_a, rotation HER_β, scaling HES_γ and mirroring HEM_β of a half ellipse are defined as follows:*

$$HET_a : \begin{cases} HE \to HE \\ (e, B) \mapsto (ET_a(e), \{T_a(x) | x \in B\}) \end{cases}$$

$$HER_\beta : \begin{cases} HE \to HE \\ (e, B) \mapsto (ER_\beta(e), \{R_\beta(x) | x \in B\}) \end{cases}$$

$$HES_\gamma : \begin{cases} HE \to HE \\ (e, B) \mapsto (ES_\gamma(e), \{S_\gamma(x) | x \in B\}) \end{cases}$$

$$HEM_\beta : \begin{cases} HE \to HE \\ (e, B) \mapsto (EM_\beta(e), \{M_\beta(x) | x \in B\}) \end{cases}$$

Lemma 3.21 *For $a \in \mathbb{R}^2, \beta \in \mathbb{R}, \gamma \in (0, \infty)$ we get*

$$(e, B) \in HE \implies \begin{cases} G^2(HET_a(e, B)) = G^2(e, B) \\ G^2(HER_\beta(e, B)) = G^2(e, B) \\ G^2(HES_\gamma(e, B)) = G^2(e, B) \\ G^2(HEM_\beta(e, B)) = G^2(HEM_0(e, B)) \end{cases}$$

3.4.3 Code Point Determination

Now the representation of a single half ellipse is going to be made robust to perspective change. At first the description of how the code point alters with perspective change will be delivered. In the next step the velocity of this modification will be investigated. At last the minimal coverage of the perspective hemisphere for a half ellipse will be constructed.

This subsection describes, how perspective change alters bow point representation. Unfortunately it is not enough just to map the bow point by means of camera model matrix.

Definition 3.26 *For $(\alpha, \beta) \in (0, \pi) \times \mathbb{R}$ the half ellipse projection $HEP_{\alpha,\beta}$ is defined as follows:*

$$HEP_{\alpha,\beta} : \begin{cases} HE \to E \times P(\mathbb{R}^2) \\ (e, B) \mapsto \left(\begin{pmatrix} P_{\alpha,\beta}(e_1) \\ P_{\alpha,\beta}(e_2) \end{pmatrix}, \{P_{\alpha,\beta}(x) | x \in B\} \right) \end{cases}$$

Lemma 3.22

$$\forall (\alpha, \beta) \in (0, \pi) \times \mathbb{R} : HEP_{\alpha,\beta} : HE \to HE$$

Lemma 3.23 *For*

$$(a, b) \in (0, \infty) \times (0, \infty)$$

and $\beta, t \in \mathbb{R}$ with

$$\cos \angle \left(\begin{pmatrix} a \cos t \\ b \sin t \end{pmatrix}, \begin{pmatrix} \cos \beta \\ \sin \beta \end{pmatrix} \right) = 1$$

we get

$$\left\| \begin{pmatrix} a \cos t \\ b \sin t \end{pmatrix} \right\| = \sqrt{\frac{1}{\frac{\cos^2 \beta}{a^2} + \frac{\sin^2 \beta}{b^2}}}.$$

Proof: Obvious as

$$\begin{pmatrix} a \cos t \\ b \sin t \end{pmatrix} = \left\| \begin{pmatrix} a \cos t \\ b \sin t \end{pmatrix} \right\| \begin{pmatrix} \cos \beta \\ \sin \beta \end{pmatrix}$$

and

$$\frac{a^2 \cos^2 t}{a^2} + \frac{b^2 \sin^2 t}{b^2} = 1.$$

$\square$

3.4. COMBINATIONS OF HALF ELLIPSES

Lemma 3.24 *For*

$$(a,b,t_0,\delta) \in [0,\infty) \times [0,\infty) \times \mathbb{R} \times \{-1,1\} \text{ with } a+b \neq 0$$

as well as

$$(e,B) = HEP(a,b,t_0,\delta)$$

and $(\alpha, \beta) \in (0,\pi) \times \mathbb{R}$ *we have*

$$\cos \angle \left(R_\beta(e_1), \begin{pmatrix} 1 \\ 0 \end{pmatrix} \right) = 1 \Rightarrow G^2(HEP_{\alpha,\beta}(e,B)) = \begin{pmatrix} 1 & 0 \\ 0 & \sin \alpha \end{pmatrix} G^2(e,B).$$

Lemma 3.25 *For*

$$(a,b,t_0,\delta) \in [0,\infty) \times [0,\infty) \times \mathbb{R} \times \{-1,1\} \text{ with } a \neq b,\ a+b \neq 0$$

and

$$x = \left\| \begin{pmatrix} a \cos t_0 \\ b \sin t_0 \end{pmatrix} \right\|$$

we get

$$\cos^2 t_0 = \frac{x^2 - b^2}{a^2 - b^2}.$$

Proof: Obvious as

$$a^2 \cos^2 t_0 + b^2 \sin^2 = x^2.$$

$\square$

Lemma 3.26 *For*

$$(a,b,t_0) \in (0,\infty) \times (0,\infty) \times \mathbb{R}$$

as well as

$$x : \begin{cases} \mathbb{R} \to \mathbb{R}^2 \\ t \mapsto \begin{pmatrix} a \cos t \\ b \sin t \end{pmatrix} \end{cases}$$

and $t_1 \in \mathbb{R}$ *with* $\langle x(t_0), x(t_1) \rangle = 0$ *we get*

$$\|x(t_1)\| = \frac{\|x(t_0)\|}{\sqrt{\frac{b^2 \sin^2 t_0}{a^2} + \frac{a^2 \cos^2 t_0}{b^2}}}.$$

Lemma 3.27 *For*
$$(a, b, t_0, \delta) \in [0, \infty) \times [0, \infty) \times \mathbb{R} \times \{-1, 1\} \text{ with } a + b \neq 0$$
as well as
$$x : \begin{cases} [0, \pi] \to \mathbb{R}^2 \\ t \mapsto \begin{pmatrix} a\cos(t_0 + \delta t) \\ b\sin(t_0 + \delta t) \end{pmatrix} \end{cases}$$
and $(\alpha, \beta) \in (0, \pi) \times \mathbb{R}$ *set*
$$y : \begin{cases} [0, \pi] \to \mathbb{R} \\ t \mapsto \langle P_{\alpha,\beta}(x(0)), P_{\alpha,\beta}(x(t)) \rangle \end{cases}$$
and
$$u = G^2(HEP(a, b, t_0, \delta)), v = G^2(HEP_{\alpha,\beta}(HEP(a, b, t_0, \delta)))$$
then we get
$$SIGNUM(v_1) = SIGNUM(y'(0)), \ SIGNUM(v_2) = SIGNUM(u_2).$$

Task 3.4 *Knowing*
$$(a, b) \in (0, \infty) \times (0, \infty) \text{ with } a \neq b$$
and
$$x_0 \in \mathbb{R} \text{ with } \exists t_0 \in \mathbb{R} : x_0 = \left\| \begin{pmatrix} a\cos t_0 \\ b\sin t_0 \end{pmatrix} \right\|$$
determine $G^1(e, B)$ *for* $(e, B) = HEP(a, b, t_0, \delta)$ *with* $\delta \in \{-1, 1\}$ *arbitrary.*

Implementation: Determine
$$\cos^2 t_0$$
with Lemma 3.25. Using Lemma 3.26 determine x_1 with
$$\exists t_1 \in \mathbb{R} : \left\langle \begin{pmatrix} a\cos t_0 \\ b\sin t_0 \end{pmatrix}, \begin{pmatrix} a\cos t_1 \\ b\sin t_1 \end{pmatrix} \right\rangle = 0 \wedge x_1 = \left\| \begin{pmatrix} a\cos t_1 \\ b\sin t_1 \end{pmatrix} \right\|.$$
Then according to Lemma 3.14
$$G^1(e, B) = \begin{pmatrix} \frac{ab}{x_0 x_1} \\ \frac{ab}{x_0^2} \end{pmatrix}.$$

$\square$

3.4. COMBINATIONS OF HALF ELLIPSES

Task 3.5 *For*
$$(a, b, t_0, \delta) \in [0, \infty) \times [0, \infty) \times \mathbb{R} \times \{-1, 1\}$$
with
$$\left\| \begin{pmatrix} a \cos t_0 \\ b \sin t_0 \end{pmatrix} \right\| > 0$$
and $(\alpha, \beta) \in (0, \pi) \times \mathbb{R}$ determine
$$G^2(HEP_{\alpha,\beta}(HEP(a, b, t_0, \delta))).$$

Implementation: Without loss of generality assume
$$ab \neq 0, \ a \neq b.$$
For
$$x : \begin{cases} \mathbb{R} \to \mathbb{R}^2 \\ t \mapsto \begin{pmatrix} a \cos t \\ b \sin t \end{pmatrix} \end{cases}$$
and with Lemma 3.23 we get $x_0 \in \mathbb{R}$ with
$$\exists s_0 \in \mathbb{R} : \ \|x(s_0)\| = x_0 \ \wedge \cos\left(x(s_0), \begin{pmatrix} \cos -\beta \\ \sin -\beta \end{pmatrix}\right) = 1.$$
Using Task 3.4 find $G^1(e, B)$ for
$$(e, B) = HEP(a, b, s_0, \delta).$$
Lemma 3.24 shows that
$$G^1(\tilde{e}, \tilde{B}) = \begin{pmatrix} 1 & 0 \\ 0 & \sin \alpha \end{pmatrix} G^1(e, B)$$
with
$$(\tilde{e}, \tilde{B}) = HEP_{\alpha,\beta}(e, B).$$
Using Lemma 3.20 determine
$$(\tilde{a}, \tilde{b}) \in (0, \infty) \times (0, \infty)$$
with
$$\exists \tilde{s}_0, \tilde{\beta} \in \mathbb{R} : (\tilde{e}, \tilde{B}) = HER_{\tilde{\beta}}(HEP(\tilde{a}, \tilde{b}, \tilde{s}_0, \delta))$$
Using Task 3.4 determine
$$G^1(HEP_{\alpha,\beta}(HEP(a, b, t_0, \delta))).$$
Using Lemma 3.27 determine
$$G^2(HEP_{\alpha,\beta}(HEP(a, b, t_0, \delta))).$$

$\square$

Definition 3.27 *For $(a, \gamma, \beta) \in \mathbb{R}^2 \times (0, \infty) \times \mathbb{R}$ half ellipse transformation $HET_{a,\gamma,\beta}$ is defined as follows:*

$$HET_{a,\gamma,\beta} : \begin{cases} HE \to HE \\ (e, B) \mapsto \left(\begin{pmatrix} T_a \circ S_\gamma \circ R_\beta(e_1) \\ T_a \circ S_\gamma \circ R_\beta(e_2) \end{pmatrix}, \{T_a \circ S_\gamma \circ R_\beta(x) | x \in B\} \right) \end{cases}$$

Finally it is possible to determine how perspective change alters bow point of a half ellipse.

Task 3.6 *For $(e, B) \in HE$ and $(\alpha, \beta) \in (0, \pi) \times \mathbb{R}$ determine*

$$G^2(HEP_{\alpha,\beta}(e, B)).$$

Implementation: As for

$$(a, b, t_0, \delta) \in [0, \pi) \times [0, \pi) \times \mathbb{R} \times \{-1, 1\}$$

and

$$(c, \gamma, \lambda) \in \mathbb{R}^2 \times (0, \infty) \times \mathbb{R}$$

with

$$(e, B) = HET_{c,\gamma,\lambda}(HEP(a, b, t_0, \delta))$$

we have

$$G^2(HEP_{\alpha,\beta}(e, B)) = G^2(HEP_{\alpha,\beta+\lambda}(HEP(a, b, t_0, \delta)))$$

use Task 3.5 to determine

$$G^2(HEP_{\alpha,\beta+\lambda}(HEP(a, b, t_0, \delta))).$$

$\square$

3.4.4 Code Point Velocity

The key point of gaining perspective robustness of the bow point representation is construction of the minimal coverage of a hemisphere segment - strategy known from the representation of straight edge combinations. The main challenge thereby is to find out how fast a code point changes through alteration of the view point. The following subsection aims to determine the velocity of this process.

Definition 3.28 *For $(e, B) \in HE$ the function $G^3_{(e,B)}$ is defined as follows:*

$$G^3_{(e,B)} : \begin{cases} (0, \pi) \times \mathbb{R} \to \mathbb{R}^2 \\ (\alpha, \beta) \mapsto G^3(HEP_{\alpha, \beta}(e, B)) \end{cases}$$

Lemma 3.28 *For $(e, B) \in HE$ we have*

$$\left(\exists x \in B : \left(F^2_{\frac{e_1+e_2}{2}, \, e_1}(x) \right)_1 > 1 \right) \Leftrightarrow G^2_1(e, B) > 0$$

and

$$\left(\exists x \in B : \left(F^2_{\frac{e_1+e_2}{2}, \, e_1}(x) \right)_1 < -1 \right) \Leftrightarrow G^2_1(e, B) < 0.$$

Lemma 3.29 *For $f, g : [a, b] \to \mathbb{R}$ continuous and $\varepsilon > 0$ with*

$$\max_{t \in [a,b]} |f(t) - g(t)| \leq \varepsilon$$

we have

$$\left| \max_{t \in [a,b]} |f(t)| - \max_{t \in [a,b]} |g(t)| \right| \leq \varepsilon.$$

Proof: Considering

$$\max_{t \in [a,b]} |g(t)| \leq \max_{t \in [a,b]} (|g(t) - f(t)| + |f(t)|) \leq \varepsilon + \max_{t \in [a,b]} |f(t)|$$

and

$$\max_{t \in [a,b]} |f(t)| \leq \varepsilon + \max_{t \in [a,b]} |g(t)|$$

we get

$$-\varepsilon \leq \max_{t \in [a,b]} |g(t)| - \max_{t \in [a,b]} |f(t)| \leq \varepsilon.$$

$\square$

Lemma 3.30 *For $f_{1/2}: [a,b] \to \mathbb{R}$ continuous with*
$$f_{1/2}(a) = 1, \ f_{1/2}(b) = -1$$
choose $t_{1/2} \in [a,b]$ with
$$|f_{1/2}(t_{1/2})| = \max_{t \in [a,b]} |f_{1/2}(t)|.$$
If we have
$$(\exists t \in [a,b]: f_{1/2}(t) > 1) \Leftrightarrow f_{1/2}(t_{1/2}) > 1$$
$$\wedge$$
$$(\exists t \in [a,b]: f_{1/2}(t) < 1) \Leftrightarrow f_{1/2}(t_{1/2}) < 1$$
then for $\varepsilon > 0$ we get
$$\max_{t \in [a,b]} |f_1(t) - f_2(t)| \leq \varepsilon \Rightarrow$$
$$|(f_1(t_1) - SIGNUM(f_1(t_1))) - (f_2(t_2) - SIGNUM(f_2(t_2)))| \leq 2\varepsilon.$$

Proof: Ass for $f_1(t_1) \cdot f_2(t_2) > 0$ the statement is obvious assume
$$f_1(t_1) > 1, \ f_2(t_2) < -1.$$
It will be shown now $f_1(t_1) - 1 \leq \varepsilon$:
$$f_1(t_1) - 1 > \varepsilon \Rightarrow f_2(t_1) > 1 \Rightarrow f_2(t_2) > 1$$
Similarly we get
$$-1 - f_2(t_2) \leq \varepsilon.$$
Finally
$$|(f_1(t_1) - SIGNUM(f_1(t_1))) - (f_2(t_2) - SIGNUM(f_2(t_2)))|$$
$$\leq |f_1(t_1) - 1| + |f_2(t_2) + 1| \leq 2\varepsilon.$$
$\square$

Theorem 3.2 *For $(e, B) \in HE$ set*
$$m = G^1(e, B).$$
For
$$(\alpha_{1/2}, \beta_{1/2}) \in (0, \pi) \times \mathbb{R} \text{ and } \zeta > 0$$
with
$$|\alpha_1 - \alpha_2|, |\beta_1 - \beta_2| \leq \zeta, \alpha_1 + \zeta < \pi$$
we get
$$\left\| G^3_{(e,B)}(\alpha_1, \beta_1) - G^3_{(e,B)}(\alpha_2, \beta_2) \right\|_{\max} \leq \frac{8\zeta|m|}{\sin^4(\alpha_1 + \zeta)}.$$

3.4. COMBINATIONS OF HALF ELLIPSES

Proof: Without loss of generality let us assume that $(e, B) = HEP(a, b, t_0, \delta)$ for
$$(a, b, t_0, \delta) \in [0, \infty) \times [0, \infty) \times \mathbb{R} \times \{-1, 1\}.$$

For
$$x : \begin{cases} [0, \pi] \to \mathbb{R}^2 \\ t \mapsto \begin{pmatrix} a\cos(t_0 + \delta t) \\ b\sin(t_0 + \delta t) \end{pmatrix} \end{cases}$$

set
$$y^{1/2} : \begin{cases} [0, \pi] \to \mathbb{R}^2 \\ t \mapsto P_{\alpha_{1/2}, \beta_{1/2}}(x(t)) \end{cases}$$

and
$$z^{1/2} : \begin{cases} [0, \pi] \to \mathbb{C} \\ t \mapsto \frac{y_{1/2}(t)}{y_{1/2}(0)} \end{cases}$$

For $t_1^{1/2}, t_2^{1/2} \in [0, \pi]$ with
$$\left| z_1^{1/2}(t_1^{1/2}) \right| = \max_{t \in [0,\pi]} \left| z_1^{1/2}(t) \right|, \quad \left| z_2^{1/2}(t_2^{1/2}) \right| = \max_{t \in [0,\pi]} \left| z_2^{1/2}(t) \right|$$

we obviously have
$$G^3_{(e,B)}(\alpha_{1/2}, \beta_{1/2}) = \begin{pmatrix} z^{1/2}(t_1^{1/2}) - SIGNUM(z^{1/2}(t_1^{1/2})) \\ z^{1/2}(t_2^{1/2}) \end{pmatrix}.$$

Corollary 3.3 shows that
$$\max_{t \in [0,\pi]} \left\| z^1(t) - z^2(t) \right\|_{\max} \leq \frac{4\zeta \|m\|}{\sin^4(\alpha_1 + \zeta)}$$

Considering previous Lemmas we finally get
$$\left\| G^3_{(e,B)}(\alpha_1, \beta_1) - G^3_{(e,B)}(\alpha_2, \beta_2) \right\|_{\max} \leq \frac{8\zeta \|m\|}{\sin^4(\alpha_1 + \zeta)}.$$

□

3.4.5 Code Point Net

This subsection finally describes how the perspective net has to be spanned to make bow point representation robust to view point alteration. The purpose is to consume as less storage and to cover as large surface of the perspective hemisphere as possible. Having the previous section just the last trivial step has to be done to achieve this goal.

Lemma 3.31 *For $\varepsilon > 0, \gamma \in [0, \pi/2), C > 0$ build the net*

$$N^C_{\frac{\varepsilon}{2},\gamma} = (\alpha_n, (\beta^n_m)_{m \in \{1,...,M_n\}})_{n \in \{0,...,N\}}.$$

For $(e, B) \in HE$ with $\|G^2(e, B)\| \leq C$ we have

$$\forall (\alpha, \beta) \in [\pi/2 - \gamma, \pi/2 + \gamma] \times \mathbb{R} \ \exists (n, m) \in \{0, ..., N\} \times \{1, ..., M_n\}:$$

$$\left\|G^3_{(e,B)}(\alpha, \beta) - G^3_{(e,B)}(\alpha_n, \beta^n_m)\right\|_{\max} \leq \varepsilon.$$

Proof: For $\tilde{\beta} \in [0, 2\pi]$ with

$$\exists n \in \mathbb{Z}: \tilde{\beta} + 2n\pi = \beta$$

we get by construction of $N^C_{\frac{\varepsilon}{2},\gamma}$ that

$$\exists (n, m) \in \{0, ..., N\} \times \{1, ..., M_n\}: |\alpha - \alpha_n|, |\tilde{\beta} - \beta^n_m| \leq \delta_n.$$

Finally

$$\left\|G^3_{(e,B)}(\alpha, \beta) - G^3_{(e,B)}(\alpha_n, \beta^n_m)\right\|_{\max} = \left\|G^3_{(e,B)}(\alpha, \tilde{\beta}) - G^3_{(e,B)}(\alpha_n, \beta^n_m)\right\|_{\max}$$

$$\leq \frac{8\delta_n \|G^2(e, B)\|}{\sin^4(\alpha_n + \delta_n)} \leq 2 \cdot \frac{4\delta_n C}{\sin^4(\alpha_n + \delta_n)} \leq 2 \cdot \frac{\varepsilon}{2}.$$

$\square$

With the new net, one can easily modify the algorithm $A^5_{\varepsilon,c,\gamma}$ to make it able to compare combinations of half ellipses. The new representation is invariant to rotation, scaling, translation and reflection. Additionally, the representation is robust to perspective change and partial occlusion. Actually, it was the goal of the Chapter 3 and the central task of the thesis to build such a representation. Now it is achieved.

Chapter 4

Extraction of Half Ellipses

4.1 Basic Idea

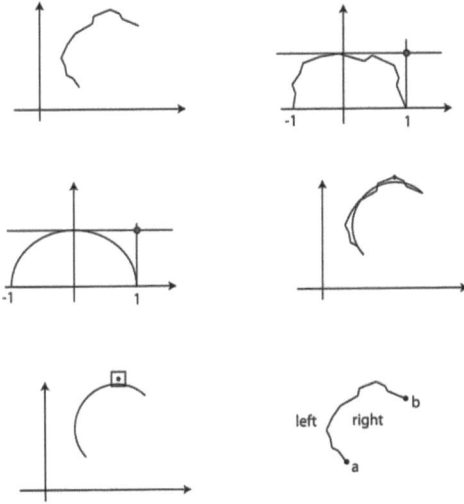

Figure 4.1: Outline of Half Ellipse Extraction

Figure 4.1 shows a draft of half ellipse detection. To find out, whether a curve is a half ellipse the system finds its bow point. In the second step the perfect half ellipse with the same bow and end points has to be determined. In the next step it is to verify whether the curve lies in a predefined neighborhood of a half ellipse with respect to maximum norm. At the end color on the both sides of the curve gets extracted.

4.2 Edge Detection

Only in this chapter, the terms edge and line are going to be distinguished. A line stands for a line section connecting two points. An edge stands for the side of a pixel. As next the new concept of an edge will be introduced in a more detailed way.

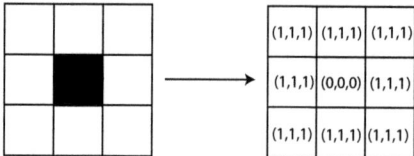

Figure 4.2: A 3×3 pixel grid. One black pixel with RGB values $(0,0,0)$ at the center. Other pixels are white and have RGB values $(1,1,1)$.

A pixel corner will be denoted as a vertex Figure 4.3. An edge is a pair

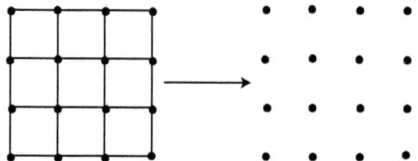

Figure 4.3: The set of vertexes of the pixel grid.

of neighbored vertexes. There are horizontal and vertical edges Figure 4.4.

Now it will be described how vertical contrast edges are detected. The horizontal ones are getting detected in exactly the same way after having transposed the pixel grid. Each line is getting processed separately. A line of pixels is a sequence of RGB vectors $(p_i)_{i \in \{1,...,n\}} \subseteq \mathbb{R}^3$. For $1 \leq i < j \leq n$ contrast intensity $CI(i,j)$ is defined as

$$CI(i,j) = \frac{\|p_j - p_i\|}{j - i + 2} - \left(\sum_{k=i}^{j-1} \|p_{k+1} - p_k\| - \|p_j - p_i\| \right). \quad (4.1)$$

4.2. EDGE DETECTION

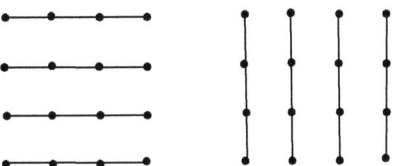

Figure 4.4: Horizontal and vertical edges.

The first term $\frac{\|p_j - p_i\|}{j-i+2}$ says the contrast intensity is the higher the bigger the difference and shorter transition is. Number 2 or generally $j - i + 2$ is chosen heuristically. This choice is due to adapt the edge detection to human visual perception. The second term $\sum_{k=i}^{j-1} \|p_{k+1} - p_k\| - \|p_j - p_i\|$ is due to diminish

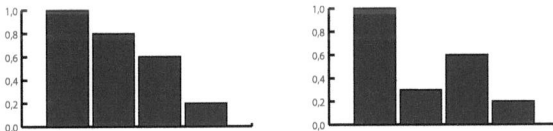

Figure 4.5: Good(left) and bad(right) transition of the red RGB component in a line.

the contrast intensity in case of a "bad" transition as showed in Figure 4.5. In case of a "good" transition the term is equal zero otherwise it is positive.

The first step of edge detection is to find $1 \leq i < j \leq n$ pairs with

$$i \leq k < l \leq j \Rightarrow CI(k,l) \leq CI(i,j) \qquad (4.2)$$

In other words contrast intensity of (i,j)-transition should be bigger than contrast intensity of any inner transition. An (i,j)-transition satisfying 4.2 will be denoted as (i,j)-true transition. In the second step such (i,j)-true transitions have to be excluded for which a (k,l)-transition exists with

$$k < i < j \leq l \vee k \leq i < j < l. \qquad (4.3)$$

In the next step a central edge has to be extracted from an (i,j)-transition as Figure 4.6 shows. In the last step each side of the extracted edge gets a RGB value. An edge is defined as an ordered pair of vertexes. Having the first and the second vertex an edge gets the left and the right side. As Figure 4.7 shows the left side of the edge gets the RGB value of the left outer pixel of a transition. The right side - that of the right outer one.

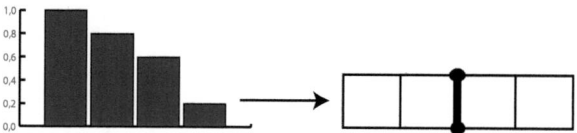

Figure 4.6: An edge at the center of a transition

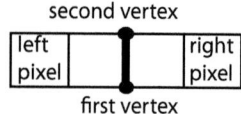

Figure 4.7: Color extraction for an edge.

4.3 Line Detection

At first a heuristic way to check if three discrete points "build" a line will be introduced. For the well known Manhattan norm $\|\cdot\|_M$ defined as

$$\|a\|_M = \sum_{i=1}^{2} |a_i| \qquad (4.4)$$

three vertices a, b, c build a line or $line(a, b, c) = 1$ if

$$\|c - a\|_M = \|c - b\|_M + \|b - a\|_M \qquad (4.5)$$

and

$$\left| \frac{\|b - a\|_M}{\|c - a\|_M} |c.x - a.x| - |b.x - a.x| \right| \leq 1. \qquad (4.6)$$

The last term can be formulated as integer multiplication

$$\|c.x - a.x\|\|b - a\|_M - |b.x - a.x|\|c - a\|_M| \leq \|c - a\|_M. \qquad (4.7)$$

A line is defined as an ordered sequence of edges $(v_1^i, v_2^i)_{i \in \{1,...,n\}} \in \prod_{i \in \{1,...,n\}} \mathbb{R}^2 \times \mathbb{R}^2$. To checks if a point p lies on a line the algorithm takes the first point of the line $first$ and tests for every vertex v_j^i of every edge if $line(first, v_j^i, p) = 1$. To check if an edge (p, q) lies on a line $(v_1^i, v_2^i)_{i \in \{1,...,n\}}$ both vertexes p, q of the edge get tested if they lie on the line. Finally $line(begin, p, q) = 1$ has to be true.

4.4. MAKING LINE CHAINS

The process of line detection is the process of line proceeding. A typical situation is: a line is given; it has to be checked if there is an edge in direct neighborhood of the last point of the line which lies on the line in the sense defined above; if so a new edge gets added to the line. Initially a line consists of a single edge. The purpose is to proceed it maximally.

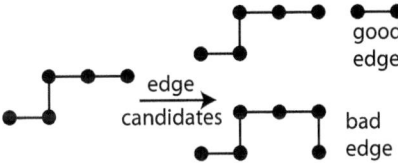

Figure 4.8: Two edge candidates to proceed a line. The bad one offends the first condition (4.5) of the line test.

4.4 Making Line Chains

Segmentation of a curve in lines is normally used to describe its form [Fre61], [DGR83], [RDLR11]. The process of composition of a curve from lines is inverse to the segmentation. Its purpose is detection of an intuitively coherent curve.

Last section delivers a set of lines. The purpose of this section is to combine them to chains. Surely, there are a lot of possible ways. To avoid the unnecessary details the most trivial one will be described.

To initialize a chain one line has to be selected randomly. A chain now consists of this one line. One of the endpoints of the initial line gets chosen arbitrarily. Let it be denoted as p. Than a set of all lines with one endpoint in some neighborhood of p has to be built. If the set is not empty a line $\tilde{l}$ has to be selected with for example the angle between l and $\tilde{l}$ closest to $180°$. The selected line $\tilde{l}$ should be added to the chain and the procedure should be repeated for the remaining endpoint of $\tilde{l}$. The procedure must be iterated until the chain can not be proceeded any more. The entire process has to be replicated for the remaining end point of the initial line l.

One line can be part of only one chain. After having been chosen a line gets tagged as a used one and can not be used any more. It is due to reduce the number of produced chains and therefore run time.

The next chain should be initialized with a line untagged as a used one.

4.5 Detection of a Half Ellipse with Color

This section shows how to check whether a chain of lines is a half ellipse. A chain should be interpreted as a pair $(e, B) \in \mathbb{C}^2 \times P(\mathbb{C})$. e_1, e_2 are the endpoints of the line chain. $B \subseteq \mathbb{C}$ consists of all points of the chain.

Now $(a, b, t_0, \delta) \in [0, \infty) \times [0, \infty) \times \mathbb{R} \times \{-1, 1\}$ and $(c, \beta) \in \mathbb{C} \times \mathbb{R}$ must be found for which the corresponding half ellipse $(e, \tilde{B})$ would have $G^2(e, \tilde{B}) = G^2(e, B)$. At first $G^1(e, B) = M \in \mathbb{C}$ has to be determined. It is trivial to calculate as $x \in B$ just have to be inserted in $F^2_{\frac{e_1+e_2}{2}, e_1}(\cdot)$. For

$$c = \sqrt{\frac{(M_1^2 + M_2^2) + \sqrt{(M_1^2 + M_2^2)^2 - 4M_2^2}}{2}} \qquad (4.8)$$

and

$$d = \sqrt{\frac{(M_1^2 + M_2^2) - \sqrt{(M_1^2 + M_2^2)^2 - 4M_2^2}}{2}} \qquad (4.9)$$

it can be shown that a can be chosen as $\frac{\|e_1-e_2\|}{2}c$, b as $\frac{\|e_1-e_2\|}{2}d$. It is known that

$$\cos^2 t_0 = \frac{1 - d^2}{c^2 - d^2}. \qquad (4.10)$$

For $t = \arctan(\sin t_0 / \cos t_0)$ set $t_0 = -t$ if $G^2_{1/2}(e, B) \geq 0$ or $G^2_{1/2}(e, B) \leq 0$. Otherwise set $t_0 = t$. If $G^2_2(e, B) \geq 0$ than $\delta = 1$ otherwise $\delta = -1$.

The system says (e, B) is a half ellipse if all $x \in B$ lay in some ε-neighborhood of $(\tilde{e}, \tilde{B})$ with respect to maximum norm, which can be analytically determined as (a, b, t_0, δ) are known and only intersection points of four lines with the half ellipse are to be found Figure 4.1.

Similarly to an edge, a half ellipse has the first and the last point. Hence, it also has the left and the right site. A half ellipse is a sequence of lines. A line is a sequence of edges. The color of the right side of a half ellipse is set as the arithmetic mean of the right side RGB values of all edges belonging to the half ellipse. The color of the left site is set correspondingly Figure 4.9.

Finally, it is possible to extract a half ellipse with two color average values on its both sides, which was the goal of this chapter.

4.5. DETECTION OF A HALF ELLIPSE WITH COLOR

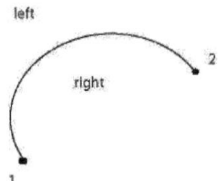

Figure 4.9: The left and the right site of a half ellipse.

Chapter 5

Flow Estimation

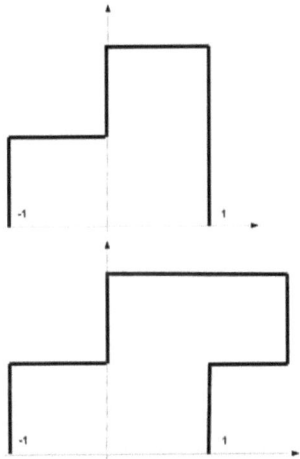

Figure 5.1: Impact of one pixel difference on the bow representation of a half ellipse.

The usage of half ellipses to estimate flow faces one major problem. Most half ellipses are so small that the representation used for object recognition is not stable enough. Figure 5.1 shows two tiny half ellipses with breadth and height less or equal 3 pixels. They appear identical to an observer under normal conditions. The invariant representation of these half ellipses is $(0, 2)^T$ and $(1, 2)$. As the ε-error-bond for bow used to validate the system is 0.2

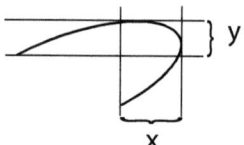

Figure 5.2: Representation vector $(x, y)^T$ of the bow of a half ellipse.

the half ellipses would not be considered as similar anymore. Whereas for a half ellipse with secant length of 20 pixels a one pixel deviation would not have any influence on recognition with bow error tolerance $\varepsilon = 0.2$. For that reason a more stable representation of the bow as shown in Figure 5.2 was chosen. For the endpoints of half ellipses a trivial translation invariant encoding was used. The disadvantage of this representation obviously is restriction to translation handling small half ellipses. With other words a combination won't be recognized after e.g. 90° rotation.

The first point of the first half ellipse of a combination should be denoted as its initial point. The translation invariant representation of the endpoints is built throw shifting of the initial point to the point of origin. The bow representation is more stable because a half ellipse does not have to be normalized. So one pixel deviation has the same impact on the representation for all half ellipses independently from the size.

Estimating flow one has to compare two frames. From the first frame the system extracts e.g. 20,000 half ellipses. For each half ellipse A a combination from some neighbored half ellipses gets built with A at the beginning. After having extracted half ellipses from the second frame the system tries to match each combination from the first frame. If the match is good enough e.g. in terms of the length of the corresponding subcombination the first half ellipse of the learned combination gets a translation vector assigned. The translation vector is built for example through subtracting of the initial points of two matched combinations. A combination from the first frame does not get compared with all combinations from the second frame. Thank to assumption that shifting of small half ellipses is small a combination A can be compared to combinations from the second frame whose initial points are in some neighborhood of the initial point of A.

In contrast to object recognition, the new flow estimator compares two combinations pairwise. The object recognition system introduced in this thesis simultaneously compares one combination with all combinations learned thanks to the new type of storage. In case of flow estimation one has to compare a combination A from the first frame with e.g. 10 combinations from the second frame in some neighborhood of the initial point of A. Building the complicated storage just for 10 combinations needs far more time than explicit pairwise comparison of A with each of the 10 combinations. The core algorithm of the comparison of two combinations robust to partial occlusion and invariant to permutations will be formulated and implemented now.

Task 5.1 *Assume $d, l_u, l_v \in \mathbb{N}$ and two combinations $u \in \prod_{i \in \{1,...,l_u\}} \mathbb{R}^d$, $v \in \prod_{i \in \{1,...,l_v\}} \mathbb{R}^d$. The task is to determine $m \in \mathbb{N}_0$ defined as*

$$m = |\{i \in \{1,...,l_u\} | \exists j \in \{1,...,l_v\} : \|u_i - v_j\| \leq \varepsilon\}| \quad (5.1)$$

with $\varepsilon > 0$. Return $m + 1$ if $\|u_0 - v_0\| \leq \varepsilon$ else 0. u, v are translation invariant representations of two combinations. They are not considered as similar if the first half ellipses are not similar.

Implementation:

```
Set<Integer> indices = new HashSet<Integer>();
for (int i = 1; i <= l_u; i++)
    for (int j = 1; j <= l_v; j++)
        if (||u_i - v_j||_max < epsilon)
            indices.add(i);
if (||u_0 - v_0||_max <= epsilon)
    return indices.size() + 1;
else
    return 0;
```

□

To propagate the flow from half ellipses to the entire plane the system checks for each pixel if there are two different half ellipses in two different cardinal direction with similar translation vectors assigned and no other half ellipses between them and the pixel. If so the pixel gets the arithmetic mean of the two translation vectors attached as the Figure 5.3 shows. If no such

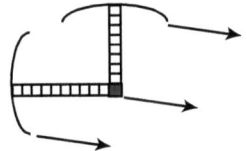

Figure 5.3: Propagation strategy.

two half ellipses are available for a pixel, the pixel gets an average translation vector of the nearest pixels whose translation vectors could be determined the way described above.

Chapter 6

Experimental Results

6.1 Color Information

Color information can be added to the pure form representation described above. Color extraction for a half ellipse was already discussed in Section 4.5. A half ellipse has a first and a last point. Hence it also has a right and a left side. After the extraction of a half ellipse the system determines arithmetic RGB average along the right side of the half ellipse as well as along the left one. Thus it determines two RGB vectors $l, r \in \mathbb{R}^3$. Color code $c \in \mathbb{R}^6$ is just Cartesian product of this two vectors $c = (l, r)$. A representation vector $a \in \mathbb{R}^{6n}$ of a half ellipse combination $b \in HE^n$ gets extended to $\tilde{a} \in \mathbb{R}^{6n+6n}$ with color code $(c_i)_{i \in \{1,...,n\}} \in \prod_{i \in \{1,...,n\}} \mathbb{R}^6$ for each half ellipse of the combination. An additional threshold value $\tilde{\varepsilon} > 0$ is used to compare the color information of two representation vectors with respect to the maximum norm.

6.2 Object Recognition

6.2.1 COIL-100

To evaluate the system the well known database COIL-100 (Columbia Object Image Library) was used. The data set is described in [NNM96]. It contains 7200 color images of 100 3D objects shown in Figure 6.1. One image is taken per 5° of rotation.

Figure 6.1: COIL-100 objects

6.2.2 Experiment Settings and Results

The computer used in the experiments has a processor Intel(R) Core(TM)2 Duo CPU P8600 @2.40 GHz 2.40 GHz and 4.00 GB RAM. The system is implemented in Java.

Basically, 2 experiments with slightly different parameter settings were made. In the first experiment 18 views(1 per 20°) were used to learn each object. The remaining 5400 images were analyzed. A recognition rate of 99.2% was reached. The time demand to learn all objects is 277 seconds. The average time demand to analyze one image is 980 milliseconds. In the second experiment 8 views(1 per 45°) were used to learn an object. The other 6400 were analyzed. A recognition rate of 96.3% was reached. The system needs 142 seconds to learn all objects. The time demand to analyze a single image is 1593 milliseconds.

6.2.3 Learning and Recognition Scheme Used for COIL-100

As mentioned above the system uses e.g. 8 images to learn an object. For one image it constructs e.g. 10 combinations of half ellipses. Each combination is represented with e.g 6 feature vectors. Each vector is labeled with the number $N \in \{1, ..., 100\}$ of the object it refers to.

Analyzing an image the system at first determines the maximal length $m \in \mathbb{N}$ of the matched subsequences for each learned feature vector. Let the set of such lengths be denoted as M. For $\tilde{m} = \max M$ the system depicts all feature vectors for which subsequences of the length $\tilde{m}$ were matched. The object with the greatest number of such feature vectors will be returned as the recognized one. Having several such objects the system chooses one of them randomly.

6.2. OBJECT RECOGNITION

6.2.4 Comparison to Alternative Approaches

The Table 6.1 is based on the results described in [YRA00], [CHPN00], [OM11]. It shows that the new approach is at least comparable to the state-of-the-art methods when solving a standard object recognition task.

Table 6.1: Comparison with Alternative Results

Method	18 views	8 views
LAFs	99.9%	99.4%
Half Ellipses	99.2%	96.3%
SNoW / edges	94.1%	89.2%
SNoW / intensity	92.3%	85.1%
Linear SVM	91.3%	84.8%
Spin-Glass MRF	96.8%	88.2%
Nearest Neighbor	87.5%	79.5%

6.3 Flow Estimation

Construction of flow estimator based on half ellipses is not over yet. It means a satisfying validation by means of a state of the art benchmark is not possible at the moment. Just a proof of principle could be delivered by now. Based on the test sequence Hydrangea of the Middlebury benchmark Figure 6.2 it could be shown that a flow estimator can be built this way. Error is 1.5 with respect to maximum norm. Time demand is 81 seconds. Extraction of half ellipses from both frames requires 79 seconds. Comparison of half ellipse combinations needs consequently just a couple of seconds.

Figure 6.2: Frame 10 of the sequence hydrangea.

Chapter 7
Summary

7.1 Comparison to Other Methods

A typical object recognition system consists of three parts:

- primary digital image processor which detects e.g. edges [Can86]

- representation vectors e.g. integral image [VJ01] and corresponding camera model e.g. pinpoint camera [Bis07]

- machine learning algorithm e.g. neural networks [Bis07]

All three parts of the approach introduced in this thesis are new. As all three parts could be used separately as components of other systems, it is worth mentioning what is new about each of them.

The half ellipse detector finds straight lines as well as cycles. In addition, its capable to find endpoints of a half ellipse, which is a serious hurdle for e.g. as hough transformation. Furthermore, the detector determines color on both sides of a half ellipse - on the one hand it works with color images in contrast to some major contemporary methods as Canny filter, on the other hand it passes the color information to the system for the further processing. The basic disadvantage of the algorithm is its running time. Detection of all half ellipses from a 500×500-image can last several minutes when using the contemporary Intel processor based Java implementation.

The new architecture of the representation vectors together with the new machine learning algorithm offer a combination of useful features. Some subset of these features can be offered by each object recognition system. Unlike other approaches the new one provides all the following properties at the same time:

CHAPTER 7. SUMMARY

- robustness to partial occlusion: the property follows from the construction of the new machine learning algorithm, experimentally it is verified as 3D objects used for validation partially occlude themselves through rotation and can still be recognized.

- robustness to affine transformations: for 2D objects the property follows from the definition of representation, experimentally it can be confirmed again as 3D objects of the benchmark COIL-100 rotate.

- robustness to deformation: the property is given, as error tolerance is a freely selectable parameter, experimentally it can be seen, because the system interprets a 3D object as a set of 2D objects with an identical label - a 2D projection of a 3D object gets deformed through rotation of this object

- combination of color with form representation: directly implemented in the system

- ability to handle not path-connected objects: the property has the same reason as the robustness to partial occlusion and follows immediately from the definition.

- an object does not have to be segmented prior to its recognition: best seen through application to optical flow estimation - thousands of combinations (objects) do not have to be segmented from each other or background in order to be recognized

- objects of varying complexity can be saved in the same storage e.g. a gummy duck and a car of COIL-100

- ability to learn several objects simultaneously: this property is anchored in the definition of the system and can be verified as the object recognition system learns 100 objects to handle the benchmark COIL-100

- the new object recognition system can be applied to flow estimation: verified experimentally

Further properties of the machine learning algorithm alone worth to be mentioned are:

- time demand to learn a new object is independent of the number of objects already learned, which makes it feasible to autonomous robotics

- algorithm is highly parallelizable: number of half ellipses extracted = number of independent threads

Special attention should be paid to the way the connection of the new representation and learning algorithm delivers such properties as cancellation of the object segmentation as a preprocessing step or robustness to partial occlusion: the system compares all combinations on an image to be analyzed with all combinations stored.

7.2 Conclusion

The experimental results presented in this thesis show first off all the general ability of the approach to handle $3D$ real world tasks. Half ellipse detection is at least stable enough to handle blurred edges of the COIL-100 images. The low resolution of the benchmark can probably be helpful for the standard methods - the new method with its special representation would definitely profit from higher resolution. Nevertheless it is still stable enough to deliver performance comparable to the state-of-the-art methods. Trivial but still noteworthy is the fact, that the system considers the color of the object in an intuitive manner without unacceptable deceleration.

High storage consumption of the system arises directly from the definition. Huge working memory of $4GB$ was fully utilize to learn just 100 objects.

Sometimes the only way to find out if an image processing technology can solve a problem is try it. The presented system might appear promising but it is too complicated to predict whether it will be able to solve every image processing task. Besides there are some principle problems not handle yet: illumination invariant color representation [DWL98], texture [HkSI73].

Similar as color, texture is a powerful device in digital image processing. It can be used for edge detection and as additional information in object description. Texture itself is an information source - it can be used to identify a human iris [Dau93]. Methods commonly used to analyze texture are: Laws technique [Law79], fractal based technique [Pen84] or Markov field based technique [HH82].

On the one hand the system is intuitively highly suitable for matching tasks as e.g. flow estimation. On the other hand dense flow estimator has not been ultimately developed yet. At the moment only a proof of principle succeeded. Face matching can be solved in various ways. Practice shows that a single class discrimination is simple enough to allow several methods to achieve almost perfect results. Far more difficult appears classification of e.g. 10000 animals photographed under arbitrary conditions. Learning and recognition scheme used for COIL 100 would definitely fail in this case. A combination of the new method with Bayes' Decision Theory [Bau02] and [Pes98] appears reasonable.

Extraction of half ellipses seems to be the greatest technical challenge for the further development of the system. On the one hand the quality of extraction still has to increase significantly. The new flow estimator detects tens of thousands of half ellipses in two corresponding frames. To achieve at least state of the art performance it should be executed with sub-pixel precision. On the other hand the detection is the predominant running time consumer during flow estimation.

Running time optimization would generally require usage of more sophisticated hardware. As half ellipse extraction has minimal working memory demand FPGA seems a good candidate for a quicker hardware implementation. Comparison of half ellipses for object recognition has hardware requirements far more difficult to satisfy. Production of code samples is perfect candidate for NVIDIA application. Further recognition process can be split in hundreds ore even thousands parallel processes which however need independent access to a rather big working memory. This is exactly the tendency of the recent years: to equip a computer with more and more independent processors and bigger and bigger working memory.

The implementation of the perspective robustness suggested in this thesis has two major disadvantages. First of all it is highly storage consumptive. Then, only a trivial and robotics irrelevant case of learning a 2D object photographed from the parallel perspective is described mathematically precisely. The actual system can still handle 3D object recognition heuristically with success. The main advantage of the implementation is: it was designed in a mathematically consistent way, which allowed to significantly reduce the number of freely selectable system parameters.

Bibliography

[ACS81] C. Arcelli, L.P. Cordella, and S.Levialdi. From local maxima to connected skeletons. *Electronics Lett.*, 1981.

[Arb90] K. Arbter. *Affininvariante Fourierdeskriptoren ebener Kurven*. PhD thesis, Technische Universität Hamburg-Harburg, 1990.

[ASBH90] K. Arbter, W. E. Snyder, H. Burkhardt, and G. Hirzinger. Application of affine-invariant fourier descriptors to recognition of 3d objects. In *IEEE Trans. Pattern Analysis and Machine Learning*, 1990.

[Bal81] D.H. Ballard. Generalizing the hough transform to detect arbitrary shapes. *Pattern Recognition*, 1981.

[Bau02] H. Bauer. *Wahrscheinlichkeitstheorie*. de Gruyter, 2002.

[BETG08] H. Bay, A. Ess, T. Tuytelaars, and L. V. Gool. Surf: Speeded up robust features. *Computer Vision and Image Understanding*, 2008.

[Bis07] C.M. Bishop. *Neural Networks for Pattern Recognition*. Oxford University Press, 2007.

[BKKS00] S. Berchtold, D. A. Keim, H.-P. Kriegel, and T. Seidl. A new technique for nearest neighbor search in. In *IEEE TKDE*, 2000.

[BP71] H.G. Barrow and R.J. Popplestone. Relational description in image processing. *Machine Intelligence*, 1971.

[BSL+07] S. Baker, D. Scharstein, J. Lewis, S. Roth, and M.J. Black R. Szeliski. A database and evaluation methology for optical flow. In *ICCV 2007*, 2007.

[Can86] J.F. Canny. A computational approach to edge detection. In *IEEE Transactions on Pattern Analysis and Machine Intelligence*, 1986.

[CHPN00] B. Caputo, J. Hornegger, D. Paulus, and H. Niemann. A spin-glass markov random field for 3d object recognition. *NIPS 2000*, 2000.

[CJT00] N. Christianini and J.Shawe-Taylor. *An Introduction to Support Vector Machines*. Cambridge University Press, 2000.

[Com94] P. Comon. Independent component analysis: a new concept? *Signal Processing*, 1994.

[CPZ97] P. Ciaccia, M. Patella, and P. Zezula. M-tree: An efficient access. In *VLDB*, 1997.

[Dau93] J.G. Daugman. High confidence visual recognition of persons by a test of statistical independence. *IEEE Trans. Pattern Anal. Mach. Intell.*, 1993.

[Dav05] E.R. Davies. *Machine Vision*. Elsevier, 2005.

[DGR83] M. Dhome, G.Rives, and M. Richetin. Sequential piecewise linear segmentation of binary contours. *Pattern Recogn.*, 1983.

[DH72] R.O. Duda and P.E. Hart. Use of the hough transformation to detect lines and curves in pictures. *Comm. ACM*, 1972.

[DT05] N. Dalal and B. Triggs. Histograms of oriented gradients for human detection. In *IEEE Conference Computer Vision and Pattern Recognition , San Diego*, 2005.

[Dun89] G. H. Dunteman. *Principal Component Analysis*. Sage Publications, 1989.

[DWL98] M.S. Drew, Jie Wei, and Ze-Nian Lee. Illumination-invariant color object recognition via compressed chromaticity histograms of color-channel-normalized images. In *ICCV*, 1998.

[FB81] M. Fischler and R. Bolles. Random sample consensus: A paradigm for model fitting with applications to image analysis and automated cartography. *Comm. of the ACM*, 1981.

[FH51] E. Fix and J.L. Hodges. Discriminatory analysis, nonparametric discrimination: Consistency properties. Technical report, USAF School of Aviation Medicine, 1951.

[FHT96] L. Fahrmeir, A. Hamerle, and G. Tutz. *Multivariate statistische Verfahren*. 1996.

[FMZ+91] D.A. Forsyth, J.L. Mundy, A. Zisserman, C. Coelho, A. Heller, and C.A. Rothwell. Invariant descriptors for 3-d object recognition and pose. *IEEE Trans. Pattern Anal. Mach. Intell.*, 1991.

[Fre61] H. Freeman. On the encoding of arbitrary geometric configurations. *IEEE Trans. Electron. Comput.*, 1961.

[FS97] Y. Freund and R.E. Schapiro. A decision-theoretic generalization of on-line learning and an application to boosting. *Journal of Computer and System Sciences*, 1997.

BIBLIOGRAPHY 93

[GKKW02] L. Gyofri, M. Kohler, A. Krzyzak, and H. Walk. *A Distribution-Free Theory of Nonparametric Regression*. Springer, 2002.

[Gut00] A. Guttman. R-trees: A dynamic index structure for spatial. In *SIGMOD*, 2000.

[Har80] R.M. Haralick. Edge and region analysis for digital image data. *Comput. Graph. Image Process.*, 1980.

[HH82] F.R. Hansen and H.Elliot. Image segmentation using simple markov field models. *Comput. Graph. Image Process.*, 1982.

[HKO01] A. Hyvaerinen, J. Karhunen, and E. Oja. *Independent Component Analysis*. Wiley, 2001.

[HkSI73] R.M. Haralick, k. Shanmugam, and I.Dinstein. Textural features for image classification. *IEEE Trans. Systems Man Cybern.*, 1973.

[Hou62] P. V. C. Hough. *Method and Means of Recognising Complex Patterns*. US Patent 3069654, 1962.

[HS81] B. Horn and B. Schunck. Determining optical flow. *Artificial Intelligence*, 1981.

[Hu62] M. K. Hu. Visual pattern recognition by moment invariants. In *IRE Transactions on Information Theory*, 1962.

[Jae05] B. Jaehne. *Digital Image Processing*. Springer-Verlag Berlin, 2005.

[KAT88] M. Kass, A.Witkin, and D. Terzopoulos. Snakes: Active contour models. *Int. J. Comput. Vision*, 1988.

[KSHC94] M.S. Kamel, H.C. Shen, A.K.C. Wong T.M. Hong, and R.I. Campeanu. Face recognition using perspective invariant features. *Pattern Recogn. Lett.*, 1994.

[Law79] K.I. Laws. Texture energy measures. In *Image Understanding Workshop*, 1979.

[Low04] D.G. Lowe. Distinctive image features from scale-invariant keypoints. *International Journal of Computer Vision*, 2004.

[LT81] B.D. Lucas and T.Kanade. An iterative image registration technique with an application to stereo vision. In *Image Understanding Workshop*, 1981.

[Luc84] B.D. Lucas. *Generalized Image Matching by the Method of Differences*. PhD thesis, 1984.

[MA08] Ye Mei and D. Androutsos. Affine invariant shape descriptors: The ica-fourier descriptor and the pca-fourier descriptor. In *ICPR*, 2008.

[Mar76] D. Marr. Early processing of visual information. *Phil. Trans. R. Soc.*, 1976.

[MH80] D. Marr and E. Hildreth. Theory of edge detection. *Proc. R. Soc.*, 1980.

[MZ92] J.L. Mundy and A. Zisserman. *Geometric Invariance in Computer Vision*. MIT Press, 1992.

[NNM96] S. A. Nene, S. K. Nayar, and H. Murase. *Columbia Object Image Library (COIL-100)*. 1996.

[OC06] F. O'Gorman and M.B. Clowes. Finding picture edges through collinearity of feature points. *IEEE Trans. Comput.*, 2006.

[OM11] S. Obdrzalek and J. Matas. Object recognition using local affine frames. *BMVC*, 2011.

[Pea01] K. Pearson. On lines and planes of closest fit to a system of points in space. *The London, Edinburgh, and Dublin Philosophical Magazine and Journal of Science*, 1901.

[Pen84] A.P. Pentland. Fractal-based description of natural scenes. *IEEE Trans. Pattern Anal.Mach. Intell.*, 1984.

[Pes98] W.R. Pestman. *Mathematical Statistics*. de Gruyter, 1998.

[PR67] J.L. Pfaltz and A. Rosenfeld. Computer representation of planar regions by their skeletons. *Comm. ACM*, 1967.

[Pra01] W. Pratt. *Digital Image Processing*. Wiley, 2001.

[Pre70] J.M.S. Prewitt. *Picture Processing and Psychopictorics*, chapter (75-149). Academic Press, 1970.

[RDLR11] G. Rives, M. Dhome, J.T. Lapreste, and M. Richetin. Detection of patterns in images from piecewise linear contours. *Pattern Recogn. Lett.*, 2011.

[Rei93] T. H. Reiss. *Recognizing Planar Objects Using Invariant Image Features*. Springer-Verlag Berlin Heidelberg, 1993.

[Ros62] F. Rosenblatt. *Principles of Neurodynamics*. Spartan, New York, 1962.

[Ros69] A. Rosenfeld. *Picture Processing by Computer*. Academic Press, 1969.

BIBLIOGRAPHY

[Rut70] D. Rutovitz. Centromere finding: Some shape descriptors for small chromosome outlines. *Machine Intelligence*, 1970.

[RZFM11] C.A. Rothwell, A. Zisserman, D.A. Forsyth, and J.L. Mundy. Canonical frames for planar object recognition. In *Proc. 2nd European Conf. on Computer Vision*, 2011.

[SA02] B. Schoellkopf and A.J.Smola. *Learning with Kernels, Support Vector Machines, Regularization, Optimization, and Beyond*. MIT Press, 2002.

[Sam89a] H. Samet. *Application of Spatial Data Structures: Computer Graphics, Image Processing and GIS*. Addison-Wesley, 1989.

[Sam89b] H. Samet. *The Design and Analysis of Spatial Data Structures*. Addison-Wesley, 1989.

[SHS03] K. Suzuki, I. Horiba, and N. Sugie. Neural edge enhancer for supervised edge enhancement from noisy images. *IEEE Tans. Pattern Anal. Mach. Intell*, 2003.

[SMP98] S. Startchik, R. Milanese, and T. Pun. Projective and illumination invariant representation of disjoint shapes. *In Special Issue on Projection Based Transforms, Image Vision Comput.*, 1998.

[SRB10] D. Sun, S. Roth, and M.J. Black. Secrets of optical flow estimation and their principles. In *CVPR 2010*, 2010.

[SU11] S. Sener and M. Uenel. Ica based normalization of 3d objects. *Multimedia content representation, classification and security*, 2011.

[TB97] Q.M. Tieng and W.W. Boles. Wavelet-based affine invariant: Representation: A tool for recognizing planar objects in 3d space. *IEEE Transactions on Pattern Analysis and Machine Intelligence*, 1997.

[Vap98] V. N. Vapnik. *Statistical Learning Theory*. Wiley, New York, 1998.

[VJ01] P. Viola and M. Jones. Rapid object detection using a boosted cascade of simple. In *CVPR*, 2001.

[WG77] R.C. Wilson and S.C. Giese. Threshold visibility of frequency gradient patterns. *Vision Res.*, 1977.

[YRA00] M. H. Yang, D. Roth, and N. Ahuja. Learning to recognize 3d objects with snow. In *ECCV*, 2000.

BIBLIOGRAPHY

Glossary

$\mathbb{C}$ Complex plane, possible representation as $\mathbb{R}^2$. 37

initial point The first point of the first half ellipse of a combination. 81

net Set of hemisphere points used to achieve robustness to perspective change. 47, 72

sample A code vector. 19, 22

i want morebooks!

Buy your books fast and straightforward online - at one of world's fastest growing online book stores! Environmentally sound due to Print-on-Demand technologies.

Buy your books online at

www.get-morebooks.com

Kaufen Sie Ihre Bücher schnell und unkompliziert online – auf einer der am schnellsten wachsenden Buchhandelsplattformen weltweit! Dank Print-On-Demand umwelt- und ressourcenschonend produziert.

Bücher schneller online kaufen

www.morebooks.de

 VDM Verlagsservicegesellschaft mbH
Heinrich-Böcking-Str. 6-8   Telefon: +49 681 3720 174   info@vdm-vsg.de
D - 66121 Saarbrücken   Telefax: +49 681 3720 1749 www.vdm-vsg.de

Printed by Books on Demand GmbH, Norderstedt / Germany